A PILGRIMAGE
of
REMEMBRANCE

The S Company Flag, presented by some good ladies in Rome, which now hangs at High House, Weasenham, Norfolk

A PILGRIMAGE
of
REMEMBRANCE

An anthology of the history of a Scots Guards Company in the
Italian Campaign 1944–45

Michael Curtis

Also incorporating passages from the Diary of Major Richard Coke DSO MC

Foreword by Professor Richard Holmes CBE TD MA PhD

Dedication

This book is dedicated to the officers and men who served with 'S' Company attached to 2nd Battalion Coldstream Guards, which later became 'B' Company 1st Battalion Scots Guards

First published in 2004 by Michael Curtis
© Michael Curtis
ISBN 0 9549044 0 0

This book is set in 11/13 point Monophoto Apollo
Designed by Robin L. Oliver
Printed by Sarum Colourview, Salisbury

Contents

Acknowledgements

I have never written a book before and to embark on this story has taken some time, coupled with much help from a good many friends. These kind people have read and re-read the draft and advised not only on the English, but also on the delivery of the actual content. It would be almost impossible to list all those who have helped, but the main contributors are: Major the Hon. Colin Dalrymple, Major General David Toler, Captain Ian Weston-Smith, Brigadier Robert Long, Lieutenant-Colonel John Darroch, Major Jim Kellie, Major Joe West (the last four from my old Regiment), Mr Geoffrey Churcher, Mr Peter Ellis, Captain Bob Clarkson and Corporal Gorman (RHQ Scots Guards) and those mentioned in the preface 'How it all began'. Mrs Anne Balfour-Fraser was enormously helpful with details of my uncle's life in England before he went to Italy. To Mrs Tommy Budgen I am most grateful for the help she gave us when we visited Warren Farm at Llandwrog.

The mechanics of producing a draft for checking have not been easy. I am most grateful to John May of Winchester for his guidance and production of the photographs. For the photocopying and binding of the initial draft and general help in putting it all together I am indebted to Oakleaf Stationery of Alresford.

I have also used some GSGS 4229 maps of 1943, with the kind permission of the Map Room at the British Library, London. I have been fortunate in being able to use some of the maps from The Scots Guards 1919–1955, with kind permission from the Regimental Adjutant.

The excerpts from Sir Ian Fraser's book, *The High Road to England*, are reproduced with the kind permission of Lady Fraser.

Finally, and no less importantly, I will be forever indebted to my wife, Rachel, and daughter, Lucinda, for typing the first draft and the even harder final version.

Michael Curtis,
Gastons, Kilmeston,
August 2004.

List of Illustrations

List of Maps

Glossary

AFHQ	Allied forces headquarters
AMGOT	Allied military government of occupied territories
AML	Air mail letter
Bde HQ	Brigade headquarters
Bn HQ	Battalion headquarters
C	Casa (house)
CCS	Casualty clearing station
Chinese attack	Feint diversion by use of fire to conceal real attack
CMF	Central Mediterranean Force
CO, 2I/C	Commanding officer, 2nd in command
Coy HQ	Company headquarters
CRU	Corps reinforcement unit
CSM	Company Sergeant Major
CQMS	Company Quarter Master Sergeant
DF	Defensive fire
Div arty	Divisional artillery
FUP	Forming up point or place
Fwd	Forward
ITRD	Infantry training and re-inforcement depot
LF, RF	Left flank, right flank
LO	Liaison officer
LOB	Left out of battle
OCTU	Officer cadet training unit
OGP	Orders group
OP	Observation post
PIAT	Projectile, infantry, anti-tank
Pl Comd	Platoon (30 men) Commander
POW	Prisoner of war
PU	Pick up (utility vehicle)
RAP	Regimental aid post
RE	Royal Engineers (sappers)
RHQ	Regimental headquarters
R & R	Rest and recuperation
Sangar	Protective wall made or rocks around a position
SB	Stretcher bearer
SP	Self propelled
Stonk	A concentration of mortar or artillery fire
TAC	Tactical HQ
TCV	Troop carrying vehicle
TEWT	Tactical exercise without troops
TSMG	Thomson sub machine gun

Foreword

It is a real pleasure to write this foreword to a book which is so evidently a labour of love and pride on its author's part. It tells the story of an infantry company in Second World War Italy, fighting grim and dangerous battles in 1944-5, at a time when events in France, Belgium and latterly Germany tended to grab the headlines. Indeed, I fear that the men who won the Italy Star the hard way have, like their comrades who fought in Burma, never really had the recognition they deserved. The project originated when Michael Curtis was sorting out his late mother's papers, and found amongst them letters about her brother, Captain Andrew Neilson, who was awarded an immediate DSO while commanding S Company but who was later mortally wounded at Monte Lignano. This discovery encouraged him to contact surviving officers who fought in or alongside S Company, and then to follow its progress from the battlefield of Cassino to the shores of Lake Comacchio where it fought its last actions.

The story of 'S' Company Scots Guards, attached to 2nd Coldstream Guards, which became B Company 1st Scots Guards in the spring of 1945 does not simply reinforce many of the old truths of infantry combat, but illuminates this one small cog in the British Army towards the end of a long war. Andrew Neilson was unquestionably a warrior, not simply a gifted trainer of men. Professor Sir Michael Howard, such a bright beacon for military historians of my own generation, won his MC as a Guards officer in Italy, thought that Neilson 'took soldiering exceptionally seriously – not only soldiering but *fighting*: not quite the same thing.' Yet Neilson was not immune to the dreadful attrition the war inflicted on his generation, writing, not long before his own death: 'One begins to wonder how and when it will all end and whether, after all, it was worth all the sacrifice.'

The company felt the full force of war's eternal caprice: in October 1944 a stray shell killed a guardsman who had won his MM in the pitched battle for Monte Piccolo, where the company had distinguished itself the previous May. And a minor action close to the very end of the war cost the company 'a first class platoon commander and a platoon sergeant.' Prisoners were welcome as a source of rather more than intelligence. An officer cheerfully reported the capture of a German sergeant: 'Loot from him consisted of a Schmeizer (sic) a pair of field glasses in not very good condition; an Iron Cross and some money.' The mill of military bureaucracy ground on, with an officer pursuing the Pay Office 'about my claim for loss of kit…about a year ago.' The Germans were generally doughty fighters. As 'S' Company carried an enemy position by assault 'the German Company Commander put up a brave but desperate resistance with his pistol, wounding several of the leading platoon, including Lieutenant Inskip, whom he shot through the eye.' Yet sometimes their bravery proved their undoing. 'I wish the Germans would put in more counter-attacks like this,' wrote an officer, 'as it is the easiest way of killing them.'

Although formal discipline was strict, there were powerful undercurrents of informal practicality. A company commander made it very clear to his commanding officer that his company had done long enough in the line: 'I pointed out to Colonel Bob very firmly that I thought we ought to be relieved tomorrow night.' Company commanders would be quietly told by their sergeant majors that 'Mr So-and-so was no good and that the men would not 'go for' him.' The process led to the replacement of platoon and company commanders. Michael Curtis, himself an experienced infantry officer, has an easy feel for his material, relating the words of Sir Ian Fraser (then a Platoon Commander) how the greatly respected Major Richard Coke had: 'a natural understanding about what commanding an infantry company was about...he had a natural feeling for landscape and ground formation and instinctively what was militarily feasible and what was not.'

And then there are war's asides. The notoriously uncomfortable seats in troop carrying vehicles; the mischance which took the company quarter-master-sergeant, complete with the men's stew, into German lines; some unexpected duck shooting.

This is an affectionate and intimate portrait of a fine rifle company. It will appeal not simply to those who have a family or regimental connection with the events it describes, but to those who wish to widen their knowledge of that perverse, tribal and enduring organisation, the British Army.

Richard Holmes

Part One

Preface

How it all began

During the last months of 2000 and the first quarter of 2001, I started a mammoth task of sorting out yet more boxes and desk drawers belonging to my late mother. The task was huge and, after about one month, the box containing papers referring to her brother was full. As children, we had been told the story of my uncle who was a wartime commissioned officer in the Scots Guards and how he had died of his wounds in Italy.

The box concerned contained an almost complete life history of Captain Andrew Neilson DSO, who commanded 'S' Company Scots Guards, attached to 2nd Battalion Coldstream Guards. I felt that I had to find out more and set about asking questions. The first of many calls was to my close friend and neighbour, Colonel Mike Smart, who was a career officer in the Scots Guards. Once he had seen the material, he suggested that I visit the Regimental Adjutant, Major Robin Whyte, Scots Guards, to tie up the loose ends. I am really most grateful to these two officers who helped enormously – Robin even produced my uncle's Personal file, which I read in Birdcage Walk, while a band played below.

I was by then convinced that I wanted to know more about 'S' Company. On departing from Birdcage Walk, Robin Whyte said that my uncle's Second in Command was alive and well and living south of Edinburgh. An overnight sleeper trip and a day spent with Major the Hon. Colin Dalrymple brought home much detail of 'S' Company, and this increased my curiosity. Further examination of the historical texts indicated that one of the officers who brought my wounded uncle down from Monte Piccolo was Captain David Toler and, thanks to Major Edward Crofton, I was able to visit him – now a retired Major General, living in Lincolnshire. A day with him was as interesting as my visit to Scotland. My mind was then made up and I put together an article based on my uncle's report on Monte Piccolo, which was published in the Scots Guards Magazine of 2002.

It was now obvious to me that 'S' company was more that just another rifle company. There appeared to be some sort of magic associated with all that it did in the year of its existence. After the death of my uncle, the company was lead by Major Richard Coke, and excerpts from his diaries are also included in this story. His son, Toby Coke, has given permission for their use and has also

1

Major Richard Coke DSO MC

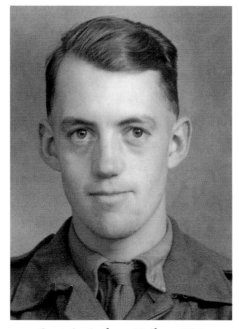

Captain Andrew Neilson DSO

Major the Hon. Colin Dalrymple

been a valuable source of information.

This anthology is based on the relevant Regimental histories, but it has a different format in that each major action is accompanied by memories of participants (where available), the 1943 maps and modern photographs taken in the period 2001 and 2003.

David Toler found amongst his documents a typed paper of some 34 pages outlining in more detail the life of 'S' Company. He does not know who wrote it or where it came from. He calculates that he must have had it since he was a Company Commander in 2nd Battalion Coldstream Guards and he does not recognise the handwriting of the corrections made. It is such a concise document that I have decided to use it for my narrative. After all, somebody else has recognised the basis of a story a long time ago and to use it will acknowledge this unknown person's efforts.

3

Part Two

Andrew Shennan Neilson 1921–1944
A Short Account of a Short Life

Andrew Neilson was born on 5 March 1921 at Barry, South Wales, the youngest child of three and only son of Dr Andrew Shennan Neilson MC, a General Practitioner, and his wife Hettie. He was sent away to prep school as a boarder at Brean House School, Weston Super Mare at the age of ten, from where he gained entry to Epsom College, a public school with a good reputation, in 1934 when he was 13.

There is no evidence that Neilson was other than a normal, bright boy, excelling in all kinds of sport (at that time deemed just as important as academic achievement) and gaining his School Certificate in ten subjects. The normal and obvious next move was to university, but there was a snag: the family fortunes were not good, and there was a financial crisis. However, as a result of support from Epsom College and charitable and other funds, he gained entry to Hertford College, Oxford, to read law. He started the Michaelmas term at Hertford in September 1939 at the age of 18, but in common with many of his contemporaries he joined up and attended basic military training at the Depot of the King's Own Yorkshire Light Infantry at Strensal, Yorkshire. He had been offered a commission in the Indian Army, but instead, at the age of 20, in August 1941, he gained an Emergency Commission as a Second Lieutenant in the Scots Guards after attending the Officer Cadet Training Unit at Sandhurst.

An account of Neilson's life would not be complete without noting that his father left home during his son's childhood. Neilson was brought up by his mother in the company of two elder sisters, and from this may stem a certain determination and desire to get done what he thought to be right.

Neilson was an excellent trainer of soldiers. In late 1943 he was involved in running the very successful Scots Guards Training Camp in North Wales, and was required to continue there after the first drafts of the Regiment had left for Italy. He caught up with his unit in early 1944.

In May 1944 Neilson was wounded in action while commanding 'S' Company attached to 2nd Coldstream Guards at Monte Piccolo, for which action he was awarded the DSO. On 16 July 1944 he was wounded in action whilst commanding 'S' Company at Monte Lignano and died later of his wounds.

He was 23.

Richard Lovel Coke 1918–2001
A Short Account of His Life

Richard Coke was born on 3 April 1918 at Weasenham, Norfolk into a landed family. His paternal grandfather was the Earl of Leicester, while his mother's father was the 14th Lord Inchiquin. He was educated at Stowe and the Royal Agricultural College at Cirencester, where in 1938 he was awarded a Gold Medal for Forestry, a subject which claimed his interest for the rest of his life. A supplementary reservist, he was mobilised in 1939 and commissioned into the Scots Guards.

After normal training in Britain, in 1943 he joined 2nd Battalion Scots Guards in the Salerno beachhead. As second in command of 'F' Company, he was involved in fierce fighting for Monte Camino, taking over the company when its commander was killed. It was largely due to his courage and example that the strongpoint he was ordered to defend was held. For his gallantry during this action he was awarded the MC.

By December 1944 Coke was commanding 'S' Company, attached to 2nd Battalion Coldstream Guards. The company formed part of the attack on Monte Penzola, with the objective of capturing the pinnacle, a feature guarded by perpendicular cliffs and liberally mined. Coke led his men to success in the fiercest of fighting and then withstood a determined German counter attack. In the words of his citation for his DSO: 'Major Coke's magnificent leadership, his complete disregard for his personal safety under heavy shell and machine gun fire, his determination ... and his heroic example had empowered his company to defeat a German battalion....'

Richard Coke ended the war in Trieste and returned home soon afterwards, the holder of a DSO and an MC at the age of 27. The management of the woods at Weasenham became his life's work and he proved it possible to combine commercial timber-growing with the fostering of ornamental trees and shrubs. He was a great countryman.

He was made Deputy Lieutenant of Norfolk in 1977 and was appointed High Sheriff for 1981. He died in 2001 at the age of 83.

CHAPTER 1

The Origins of 'S' Company, Scots Guards

Warren Farm, Llandwrog

The build up of trained men for the two Scots Guards battalions overseas was already initiated by the formation of the Training Battalion in September 1939 at Pirbright. It was to this camp that reservists were sent, together with some 300 Police reservists. Equipment and transport for training were far from adequate for the 1200 men who now made up the total strength. From this source half the number left in 1940 to form the Holding Battalion at the Tower of London and the rest, making up the Training Battalion, moved to better accommodation at Pirbright at D Lines. The training of recruits started at the Depot, where they were taught drill and small arms, after which they went to Pirbright. In the first years of the war, there was a lack of up-to-date battle experienced men among the instructors – not just for the Regiment, but throughout the Army as a whole. However, there was no lack of keenness and initiative in the cadre of instructors and new approaches to training for battle evolved, such as tank drills, street fighting and camouflage training.

Warren Farm, Llandwrog – The Scots Guards battle camp in N Wales, 2003

Clearly these early days produced good results, but the lack of battle experienced men was a problem. The formation of the School of Infantry at Barnard Castle in late 1942 provided the initiative to improve the training for battle. The staff were drawn from those who had returned from Dunkirk, after which a standard regime of training was established. To this centre were sent many young officers and NCOs who, on their return to Pirbright as instructors, passed on their knowledge to the recruits.

In the Autumn of 1943 a cadre of officers and NCOs finished a special course at Barnard Castle. It was at this time that the Training Battalion established its own battle camp at Warren Farm at Llandwrog near Carnarvon. This cadre formed the demonstration platoon at Warren Farm, conveniently situated on the edge of the Snowdon Mountain Range. It was here that field training and live firing were carried out in realistic conditions.

It was generally accepted that the development of close quarter battle exercises was improved, particularly with the Bren gun and hand grenades. The training was planned and carried out by Major Jack Sanderson, Capt. The Hon. Bill Vestey and Captain Andrew Neilson. The weather conditions were very severe and uncomfortable, which, in a private letter to a friend, Neilson described as 'cold, wet and miserable' most days. On some there was a very hard frost, but with a warm sun. He goes on to say that it was all very hard work and rather boring as well. Initially lunch was 'rather indifferent

Warren Farm. The Camp site is within the dunes shown in the background

The Scottish thistle badge at the entrance to Warren Farm battle camp, Llandwrog 2003

sandwiches', but morale was high and the men responded well, particularly when they were told in no uncertain terms that 'people like Germans do not conquer people like us'.

There were brighter moments. When there was a gap in between courses the staff went duck shooting, particularly exacting with gales off the sea. Everything was proceeding smoothly, up to the point when Bill Vestey left to go to the 1st Battalion. Andrew Neilson had to impress the skills needed more firmly to ensure that the courses continued without a hitch. He said that he had to fight like hell to get his way where the basic tactics were concerned. In the end, matters improved, helped by better weather, and by determination and delicate diplomacy.

Life must have been very hard, wet through for days and nights on end; only being comfortable back at camp in front of a roaring fire, wearing a greatcoat, after a reasonable meal. On one occasion the wind was so severe up in the mountains that they could hardly stand up. Training became too dangerous and was halted.

So important was this training that more courses were sent up, resulting in one course finishing and the next starting the following day, the short turnaround resulting in the edge going off the instruction. It was also unfortunate that several differences in policy on training cropped up, which meant that Neilson was being asked to teach various aspects which he knew to be wrong. He said he refused to do this and expected this to be his last course.

He continued, apparently when the weather had improved, to say that he always liked to see the vast improvement that took place in the first week. The Demonstration Platoons were first class in their job – 'they are the result of many hours hard and patient work. They are just about as near perfect as any body of men can be and I am always striving to make everyone else reach the same standards. Their pride in their art has become tremendous, the whole thing has become quite unmilitary – the rehearsals and stage management are terrific'.

It was from this background and training that drafts of men were sent to Italy as first class reinforcements for the two battalions serving in Italy. Large numbers of Scots Guards soldiers had been sent from Britain to the Infantry

Administrative buildings at Llandwrog 2003

Rest and recuperation camp site at San Potito where S Company joined 2nd Coldstream

Reinforcement and Training Depot (IRTD) at the village of Rotondi. This untidy village had nothing to offer by way of relaxation. There was just a large camp overlooked by the castle of Monte Sarchio on one side and dominated by Monte Tabouno on the other. At this location all reinforcements for the various infantry regiments were prepared for the day when they would go up into the line.

In March 1944, Andrew Neilson arrived at IRTD at Rotondi, where he found that the Scots Guards contingent, which now comprised some 400 men, was fit and ready. 150 of these had been trained by him at Llandwrog and were familiar with the new ideas and enthusiasm which had grown at the School of Infantry and were well known in the 4th Battalion. At Rotondi, these 150 men were under Captain Neilson and were trained as a company. It was only natural that they were kept together and formed into a rifle company, 'S' Company, whose future successes are described in this book.

At this time, the 2nd Battalion Coldstream Guards had had a hard time at Monte Ornito in the February and it was decided that the new Scots Guards Company should be posted over to make up the fourth rifle company. This, it was stated, was a purely temporary measure, but it lasted for the best part of 12 months.

Therefore, on 28 March 1944, the Company joined 2nd Battalion Coldstream Guards at San Potito. It was decided to retitle the company 'S' Company, from the first letter of its parent regiment. The proper lettering of companies went by the wayside in Italy and 'S' Company stuck for the whole of its time with 2nd Battalion Coldstream Guards. There were certain doubts as to whether the chemistry would be right and if this cross posting would be successful, but the Scots Guardsmen settled down very quickly in their new role.

The Order of Battle on formation was:-

Major H.D. Cuthbert

Captain A.S. Neilson

Lieutenant H.R. Bridgeman

Lieutenant J.W.F. Lloyd-Johnes

Company Sergeant Major T Brown.

One week after joining 2nd Battalion Coldstream Guards, 'S' Company entered the line at Cassino where the allied armies had been held up since December 1943.

A Letter to RHQ from 'S' Company:
'CAPT. A.S. NEILSON   'S' Company.   21 Apr. 44.

As you probably know far more accurately than I do what is going on out here, this letter will certainly contain no news for you.

If you hadn't already heard, you can see by the address what has happened to us – temporarily. When I arrived at the IRTD there were so many Scots Guards there that Archie Coats suggested I trained 150 men separately. I took all the men that had been at Col. Archie's Battle School and formed them into three Platoons and then quite suddenly we were rushed off here. So far we have enjoyed it immensely and have had exactly the right type of gentle baptism

How long we shall remain here is uncertain but I understand that it will be for at least another month. At the moment David Cuthbert commands us but I understand that Ronnie Rowe will shortly take over. As I had had a large share in training them and as I was the only Officer to know all the Company, I was entrusted with the job of second in command – a very bogus position that will only last as long as we are here. So far we have acquitted ourselves well enough as their youthful enthusiasm is unbelievable and the standard of N.C.Os. is very good.

After the years of training I've done I'm delighted to have the opportunity of seeing how it all works – especially with a Company of N.C.Os. and men trained on the same lines. It is early yet to form an opinion but we are all confident that the training is right if only for the tremendous confidence it produces – not only in oneself but in everyone else too.'

Details of the shoulder title as worn by S Company when attached to 2nd Coldstream

CHAPTER 2

San Potito and Cassino

'S' Company had shaken down and had one brief week to mould itself into the organisation of 2nd Battalion Coldstream Guards. San Potito is a small town on the edge of the hills due north of Capua. The base area of the Battalion was amongst olive trees in a very peaceful setting in the Volturno Valley. 'S' Company's arrival was viewed with a certain amount of trepidation – would the two different backgrounds clash and cause friction? It had been made clear by the Commanding Officer, Colonel Hugh Norman, that the addition of a full company from another Guards Regiment into his Battalion was to be made to work and be successful. There was in fact no need whatsoever for there to be any concern; 'S' Company settled down very quickly and there were no actions where 'S' Company was deployed wherein they did not give a very good account of themselves.

Cassino is situated at the end of the Liri valley along the main road from Naples to Rome – Route 6 – and was the key position in the German Winter line. Behind and above the town stands the Benedictine monastery, in a commanding position, and further behind lies the rather larger mountain of Monte Cairo. The Germans therefore had a superb view across the Liri valley from within the monastery's secure walls. As an additional factor the German front was enhanced by the protection of the Rapido river, which the Germans had caused to flood across the area around Cassino.

There had been four major battles for the Monastery – US 11 Corps in January and early February, the 2nd New Zealand and 4th Indian Divisions in mid February and the air attack of 15 March, which reduced the monastery to rubble. This enabled the NZ corps to take over most of the town. Deadlock had been reached in that the British were established on the lower slopes and men of the German 1st Parachute Division still held the Monastery position, maintaining their near perfect observation of the all important Route 6.

The whole of this town had been devastated and it was into this desperate position that 2nd Coldstream moved on 5 April. They were to spend well over a month in the area, with short spells out of the line to recover. On 5 April, after an advance party had made a complete recce, the Battalion arrived, to take the central section of 1st Guards Brigade front, facing the Continental Hotel. That night the relief of the line was completed – 2 & 3 Companies and

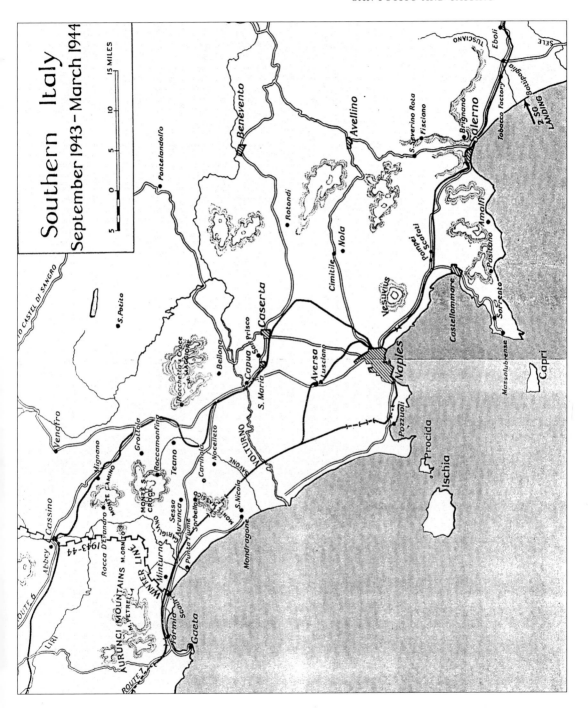

Southern Italy
September 1943 – March 1944

Bn. HQ filed up Mad Mile (so called because it was within range of the German guns) to relieve the NZ battalion. The HQ was located in a crypt which they shared with the battalion to the left (3 Grenadier Guards). After two days the Welsh Guards took over the right and with the Grenadiers on the left front, 1st Guards Brigade was now in Cassino and responsible for it.

'S' Company was held in reserve behind the Rapido River, about one mile to the rear. As one of the two companies held in rear, it perfected the drill to resupply the forward two companies and Battalion Headquarters. The area surrounding the position was completely devastated by the constant bombing. It was a sea of pieces of rubble and stinking water-filled craters and unburied bodies. Efforts were made with quicklime to deaden the putrid smell, which became much worse with the onset of better weather.

On 13 April it became 'S' Company's turn to go into forward position – they moved up and relieved 2 Company in the left forward area. This entailed moving up Mad Mile by night – an extremely difficult task owing to the fact that there were no recognizable features – it was no easier when daylight

'Mad Mile', Cassino, from the monastery 2001

appeared. 'S' Company had to live in an area dotted with sangars and protective piles of rubble, knowing all the time that the Germans were in some cases as little as a few yards away. This situation meant that all resupply had to take place by night (and sometimes under cover of smoke) and any member of the company wounded had to suffer until nightime before being evacuated. After 10 days of holding this quite dreadful position, the Battalion was relieved by a battalion of the Black Watch and, with much relief, made its way down Mad Mile to waiting transport which took them to the peace and quiet of the olive groves of San Potito. Nearly two weeks were spent in extensive training for the next offensive, which had been dubbed the Spring offensive. As was normal, 'S' Company re-equipped themselves and took the opportunity for rest and some recreation. It was during the spell in Cassino that Captain Neilson wrote of 'S' Company that 'so far we have enjoyed it immensely and have had exactly the right kind of gentle baptism to give us the all important experience'.

It was at this time that Lieutenant J.S. Wilson joined 'S' Company in place of Lieutenant Lloyd-Johnes. On 5 May the Battalion was back again in the same position under Monastery Hill – 'S' Company was again held in reserve, but for only three days, when they were moved up to their old position of some 11 days earlier. On 8th May, Lieutenant E.M. Sharp was killed by shellfire; he had only joined the company a week earlier.

In Cassino, all was much the same as before, but a new position was ordered, on Castle Hill. 4 Company (Major Palmer) took up positions under the castle walls, under the command of 3 Welsh Guards. Supply became exceedingly difficult and was by means of a steep path, some 50 yards from enemy positions, often resulting in a shower of grenades on the supply run.

Three days' stock of food had been portered up to the forward companies in preparation for the offensive, due on 11 May. 1st Guards Brigade's orders were to lean on the Germans and keep them occupied whilst the 2nd Polish Corps would cross the Rapido north of the town, and 4th and 8th Divisions would cross the River Gari to the south with the aim of surrounding the Germans.

The nightly smokescreen was deployed across the town on the evening of 11 May when, to start with, hardly a shot was to be heard. As the time for the offensive came round at 2300 hrs., the Battalion aroused themselves to await the onslaught. This started almost delicately, but suddenly became a barrage of 900 guns firing over their heads. The conditions remained the same with constant smoke screens to cover the R. Gari crossings and the roar of the guns and continuous rattle from Brigade machine guns.

17

The situation would seem to have turned on 13 May, when parties of Germans were seen to be withdrawing north on Route 6. 'S' Company helped them on their way. This resulted in higher headquarters expecting that a total withdrawal had taken place, but the Battalion's forward companies were not at all sure of this, a fact that was borne out by intense German machine gun fire on 17 May, after calls for them to surrender.

By the morning of 18 May, patrols from 4 Division entering the town from the west found it deserted and by midday 'S' Company found the whole area swarming with sightseers and reporters – until two trod on mines, which invited new German shelling. The forward platoons eventually emerged from their positions and discovered that the battlefield was much smaller than they had believed, hiding in their sangars. In the late afternoon, 2nd Battalion Coldstream Guards left the town and marched back down Mad Mile in broad daylight. It was as if a frightening nightmare had come to an end. There followed four days' rest in the area of the guns of 78 Division to recuperate and re-equip, followed by two days at three hours notice to move.

Report on Conditions in Cassino (writer unknown)
'The Battalion held the central sector of the Cassino area from the night of 5/6 April until the night of 22/23 April. Two companies and advanced Bn. HQ were in the town itself, and two reserve companies occupied positions about a mile back behind the Rapido. 3rd Battalion Welsh Guards on our right and 3rd Battalion Grenadier Guards on our left each had three companies in the town and one in reserve.

When the NZ Division attacked Cassino in March two bridges were built across the Rapido, one on route 6 and one in the area of the station. Tanks had been brought into the town and a Jeep head had been established at the Crypt, which Bn HQ were to share with 3rd Battalion Grenadier Guards. This phase did not last long and before the Battalion took over, enemy shellfire had rendered the bridges impassable except for men on foot. The tanks, nine in all, remained in Cassino during our stay. Mostly unharmed, they could not move in the rubble.

The enemy could observe our whole area from Monastery Hill and the houses below it, so that all movement had to take place by night, and in the forward company areas always under cover of smoke. The supply line for the Battalion was Route 6. Ambulance Jeeps, if called for, would come as far as the bridge across the Rapido, but no other wheeled traffic came nearer to Cassino than the Cemetery. It was from the debussing point there that the porters came forward every night. Provided it was not bright moonlight, the porters could come up as far as the Crypt without the help of smoke, but to supply the forward companies safely, a smoke screen had to be put down. This was started every evening at 2015 hrs, and porters were not allowed up to the companies until it was thick enough to cover their movement. Rations, water and ammunition were brought up in this way and supplying was usually over by 2300 Hrs, when the porters reported to the Crypt checkpoint and returned to A Echelon.

Forward of the Rapido few roads were recognisable. The road to the Crypt was only a footpath round the bomb craters but it was well worn and easy to follow. The forward companies were very hard to find, living as they did in sangars and cellars under heaps of rubble. The platoons in many cases had section or two man posts which could only be visited by night, and when two men of 4 Company were killed on the morning of April 20th, they lay undiscovered until the evening. By day each post could observe for a short way, but could probably see no more than a broken wall and the remains of a house beyond. From this meagre and unrecognisable data it was hard for companies to establish their exact positions on a large scale map or an air photograph.

Sanitary conditions were surprisingly good. There was plenty of shell hole water for washing, and the weather was not hot. In summer, Cassino will not be habitable, and the flooded fields of the Rapido valley provide a perfect breeding place for mosquitoes.'

CHAPTER 3

Monte Piccolo

After Cassino and a welcome rest period, on 25 May 1st Guards Brigade moved off in transport up Route 6 towards Rome. The next day there was a halt to allow forward platoons to mount the Sherman tanks of 17/21 Lancers, and proceed towards Arce, where German positions had been identified on a three hill feature astride Route 6, one mile short of the town. The German commander had chosen his position with some care, indeed it had probably been selected months before, and the 800 ft. slopes were in no way ideal country for attacking tanks. To the left of the road, the ridge was divided by a saddle into two halves, each about a mile in length, Monte Piccolo to the East and Monte Grande to the West. That evening the Welsh Guards reached the lower slopes of Piccolo and managed to occupy its neighbour, Monte Providero, on the other side of the road. The armour sought out fire positions on the following morning and at 4 o'clock in the afternoon, orders were given out for an immediate night attack. The Grenadiers were to go for Monte Grande whilst the Coldstream captured Monte Piccolo.

Neither Colonel Norman nor his Company Commanders had much time to examine in daylight the ground over which they were to fight, nor could any reconnaissance be made of the forming up place or of the route to it and when the Battalion set out in the inky darkness at 9 o'clock they had only their maps and compasses to guide them. 'S' and Number 3 Companies went for the main feature, which they managed to capture with considerable ease in the face of only minor opposition, and by 2 o'clock in the morning both were digging in amongst the rocks on the summit. On the left, the Grenadier attack had been equally successful, but there were still enemy on the slopes in between, who lay low in the darkness and remained unnoticed until the dawn. There were also other Germans even nearer who did not disclose themselves during the attack and when Lance Corporal Downie was sent off from Company Headquarters during the consolidation with a message for one of the platoons, he ran into a small party of them. He was quite alone, but when next seen had with him two prisoners each of whom were dragging the body of a comrade.

Despite their seeming lack of effort to defend their positions, the enemy knew what they were doing and at half past four a savage counter-attack came in on Monte Grande which drove the Grenadiers off the summit. This placed

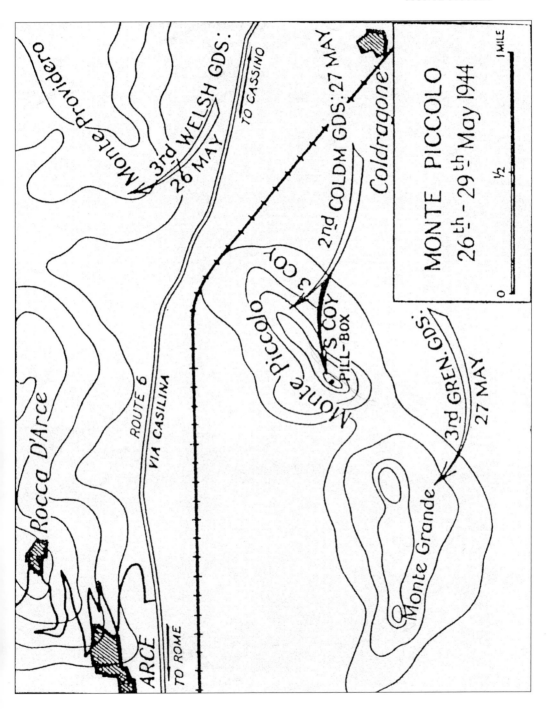

MONTE PICCOLO
26th – 29th May 1944

the Coldstream left flank, held by 'S' Company, in a rather precarious position and at 8.15 a.m. they too were attacked and No. 3 Company fifteen minutes later. The German infantry did not lack for courage in these attacks and both companies were subjected to a barrage of grenades and Schmeisser fire at very short range before the enemy could be driven off. Lieutenant Bridgeman was killed whilst commanding his platoon in this opening stage of the battle and Captain Neilson, who was in command of the Company during Major Cuthbert's absence on leave, was quite badly wounded. However, despite the fact that he was losing a good deal of blood he would not be evacuated whilst 'S' Company were still engaged with the enemy and spent the remainder of the battle walking about on the open hillside, with scant regard to his own safety, encouraging everyone by his great gallantry.

Monte Piccolo from near Coldragone, 2001

Throughout the morning, the enemy attempted to infiltrate men over the crest of Monte Piccolo and into the company positions. However, they reckoned without the skill and bravery of Lance Corporal Smythe and Guardsman Munday who spent the entire day, until finally knocked out by an S.P. Gun, in a stone sangar on the summit, thwarting all their efforts with well aimed bursts of Bren and Tommy Gun fire. About mid-day there was a lull and, whilst it lasted, the men from the reserve companies toiled up the steep slopes with water and ammunition to those who lay amongst the rocks on the top, under the blazing sun. The wounded helped each other down to the RAP and Captain Neilson even consented to go with them, only to return as soon as his wounds had been dressed despite the strongest protests of the doctor. No sooner had he completed the stiff climb back again, very weak from loss of

blood, than a second and even more determined counter-attack came in upon the 'S' Company position. For some time the whole Scots Guards area was a confused mass of hand to hand fighting with Captain Neilson in the midst doing all he could to encourage, direct and fight off the ferocious German assaults. A near miss from a shell and weakness from his wound eventually caused him to faint and once the enemy had been driven off he was carried from the field, still protesting. Lieutenant H.F.C. Charteris, who had only joined 'S' Company a fortnight before, and on whom, since from early morning he had been the only officer unhurt, a great deal of the burden of commanding the Company had fallen, now took over complete command, only to become severely wounded in the head almost at once.

With all its officers now casualties, 'S' Company finally threw the enemy off its position with the bayonet under the spirited command of Company Sergeant Major Brown who rallied the hard pressed platoons as if on the barrack square and led them in an overwhelming charge which regained the crest and drove the Germans pell mell on to the reverse slope beyond. Such enthusiasm and leadership was infectious and, dashing ahead of his platoon during this charge, Lance-Sergeant Jones, who had taken over Lieutenant Bridgeman's command, seized the barrel of a Spandau which was actually firing, pulled it towards him and, turning it upon its own crew, killed them and in one heroic act saved the lives of a number of his own men.

The enemy, driven off in such a fashion, made no further attempt to return and Company Sergeant Major Brown was able to consolidate the Company's morning positions and hold them until nightfall when Lieutenant J.S. Wilson came up to take over command. It had been a hectic day and one which caught the eye of the war correspondents, who, for once unfettered by censorship, wrote freely of the 'Epic of Piccolo Hill', an action 'which will hold a proud place in the Battle Honours of the Guards for all time'.

Forty German bodies were recovered from Piccolo after the battle, whilst 'S' Company buried one officer and seven of its men, and twenty more were wounded. For their gallantry during the action Captain Neilson was awarded a DSO, only the second such decoration to be won by a Scots Guards Company Commander at that stage of the War, and Company Sergeant Major Brown the Distinguished Conduct Medal. Lieutenant Charteris received the Military Cross and Military Medals went to Lance Sergeant Jones, Lance Corporals Downie and Smythe and to Guardsmen Munday and Lingwood; the last having been for most of the battle the only stretcher-bearer in the company area.

Report from Italy
MAJOR THE EARL OF LINDSAY.   *No. 1 IRTD.*   *4 June 44.*

The outstanding news this week is the very fine performance put up by 'S' Coy. with 2nd Battalion Coldstream Guards at Monte Piccolo during the fighting on 27/29 May. I visited both Brigades on 31 May and 1 June and everyone said the same about this company and particularly Andrew Neilson and CSM. Brown. The Brigadier praised them and then Colonel Hugh Norman and the Welsh Guards talked of it when I went to see them. Andrew carried on for hours after being wounded and then CSM Brown carried on commanding the company with great success. The casualties were:- Bridgeman killed, Andrew Neilson and Hugo Charteris wounded, seven other ranks killed and 20 other ranks wounded. Andrew was not badly wounded in the arm but lost a lot of blood. I have seen him here and he is O.K. (he escaped from hospital for a few hours). Charteris is not badly wounded. David Cuthbert was on leave at the time but has since re-joined. We have sent up, to replace casualties, Gussie Fergusson-Cuninghame as 2nd Captain, Colin Dalrymple and Jack Baxter. Gussie will be relieved by Andrew when fit. I had a great visit, going to both Brigades and all six battalions and Army Headquarters where I saw Johnny Bland. I slept the night (or rather didn't sleep the night) with Col. Hugh, as we were in the middle of the medium gun area and the noise was deafening. To my relief nothing came back! I arrived at Col. Guy's in time to see the Officers 'fall in' on a CO's. Parade – Arms Drill and march past to the Pipes. It might have been Wellington. It looked fine. Yesterday our company here sent a Guard of Honour of 60 under John Rob to Naples where Gen. Alexander was opening a new central NAAFI in the Palace. They had the Grenadier Band and it all went very well. They looked very smart. The Grenadier Band comes here this morning for three days.

S Company at Monte Piccolo 26-29th May 1944 by Terence Cuneo showing CSM T Brown crew and killing him

rallying the Company & Lance-Sergeant P Jones turning the barrel of a spandau onto its

Letter from Andrew Neilson to his fiancée, Miss Anne Balfour, from a field hospital where he was recovering from wounds received on Monte Piccolo.

3rd June, 1944

My darling Anne,

I have just finished one letter to you and now I am starting another and I will try to tell you what has been happening. As you have probably guessed, since we joined the Coldstream we have been into the line at Cassino twice, each time for about twenty days. The second time – I was left out of the battle – David and I are never in together. The company was there when the town fell although I was not there myself. Both times it was very quiet, but rather unpleasant as the smell was quite disgusting; but it served as a very useful innoculation. As soon as we came out of Cassino, we were on the move at once and spent 10 days following up behind the advance, but no actual fighting – an air attack and some shelling was all we had. David was on leave so I was commanding the company. By the time it was our turn to attack, we were worn out already and the moving up is a dreary business – no proper meals and no proper sleep for 10 days is no good for men who have just been into Cassino for 20 days! However, we were quite suddenly ordered to attack a sharp little hill at night with no time for the usual preparation. Despite all the early muddles, the attack went very well and was quite easy. But from the moment we reached the crest, we were counterattacked solidly for the rest of the night and all the next day. The country was such that all the fighting was very close – grenades and Tommy guns and it was jolly exciting. It was all amongst the rocks and quite suddenly a head would pop up a few feet away – we simply had to shoot first and hope for the best. It was just like an old cowboy film where they shoot it out amongst the rocks. The Battalion on our left was driven off the hill and the company on the right went off for a couple of hours – that was our only sticky time. The guardsmen were terrific and fought as I had never dared to hope they would. They did all the right things, sometimes without being told. The Germans were incredibly brave as most of them just committed suicide, but they did not fight well – by that I mean they had no plan and little skill but just kept fighting and we took only a few prisoners. The company is now a great success and everyone is delighted with us. We are pleased too, but most pleased am I. You can see why. You know how much trouble we had in keeping together; how many people have told us we were too young and too inexperienced and would do no good; how much trouble we had to get back our own casualties from IRTD. Now the success has finished all that. At the IRTD the other night Dickie Buckle said how right I had been and he will do all he could to help us in the future – a great triumph. My own feelings were almost nil. I had no time to think before the attack, during it and during the terrific fighting the following day, it was just like a very rough rugger match and as such quite fun. When I was coming away in an ambulance I felt as if I had been carried away from a rugger field and then suddenly I realised it was quite dangerous! The terrific catharsis now being comfortable and reflecting on it all in peace is real pleasure. Hugo was incredibly good and I have recommended him and I hope it goes through. I am sorry to have been so boring. Next time I will use a whole letter to say how much I love you.

Andrew.

David = David Cuthbert

Hugo = Hugo Charteris

A letter from Lieutenant Colonel Robert Coates CO 2nd Battalion Coldstream Guards to Andrew Neilson's sister, enclosing the account of the Battle of Monte Piccolo

CMF, December 1944.

Dear Mrs Curtis,

Many thanks for your letter of November 24th – I enclose a copy of Andrew's account of the battle of Monte Piccolo. He doesn't say how well he did himself of course, but I think one can realise what he did by reading between the lines.

'S' Company continue to do very well and in their last battle took 1 officer and 25 other ranks prisoner.

Yours sincerely, Robert Coates.

Report on Monte Piccolo by Captain A.S. Neilson

'We got off to time behind No. 3 and of course started getting tangled up with them straight away, but we veered off to the left to get away from them and found ourselves crossing the most appalling country and over an intermediate knoll (later occupied by No. 2). I asked for an extra 30 minutes stonk so that we should be close behind it, as we had lost a lot of time in thick country etc. We went up the hill with shells amongst the leading platoon (fortunately with no casualties) and got onto the crest, as the stonk lifted. We only had an odd grenade and a few rifle shots fired at us. At that stage I thought they had withdrawn and left the hill altogether, so I pushed two platoons down the forward slope about 200 yards. They met the Krauts returning – took 6 prisoners and shot a few more. I have no doubt that they had gone back off the crest while the stonk was on and were on their way back when it lifted – so it was as well we were as close to our stonk. This was confirmed in the morning when we found several Spandaus in position, cocked and ready for fire. As soon as I was sure of the feature I called back the two forward platoons to dig in on the reverse slope. While they did this we had out a strong standing patrol and the reserve platoon lining the crest. They actually had to build sangars of course. We could not go down the slope more than 10 or 12 yards, otherwise we lost sight of the crest because of the little stone walls and terraces. While it remained dark the standing patrol kept meeting odd men and the Krauts kept trying in small numbers to reach the crest. Only one of these attempts could be called a counter attack and even that was a poor attempt and easily beaten off by the platoon on the crest. As it got light I withdrew the platoon off the crest and I relied on a few observation posts to warn us, at the same time occupying the key to our whole position, which was a rubble heap, remnants of a pill box on the very left of the crest. We put a Bren and a sniper in this and another Bren beside it. With the platoon off the crest I suddenly realised that Coy HQ was in front of everyone so I gave hasty orders to move it back. While I was collecting my own staff together, a shower of grenades came over and one of them hit me in the arm. This was about 4.30 a.m. and we continued showering grenades and firing Tommies at each other for about an hour. In the meantime I had pushed two Brens round the right through the saddle and they, together with Hugo's (Charteris) two Brens in the pillbox, caused great havoc. All the morning these enemy efforts continued – they could hardly be called counter attacks, but more efforts of infiltration.

We were really fairly safe as the pill box enfiladed them completely over on their side of the crest and, if they looked really dangerous, a couple of Brens pushed forward through the saddle did the trick. Nearer than that it was grenade and Tommy gun. In the middle of the morning we thought No. 3 had been driven off, which worried us a little and I had a party struck off solely to watch the saddle, as I feared they might infiltrate between us and No. 3. One small party did but we rounded them up easily enough. We heard No. 3 ask for a reserve company to come up and then saw some streaming down the hill. As this was very shortly after we had watched the Grenadiers being driven off Grande, there were one or two worried faces, but fortunately nothing serious. Then followed a very unpleasant half hour as we had some stonking (not very heavy) and two Spandaus across our back – one from the crest and the other from somewhere on our right – I think the rocks behind No. 3. When No. 3 got back up we were much better off and we were able to sort ourselves out a bit.

We had a fairly quiet time so I went down to get my arm dressed. Up till this time (1100 hrs.) I had only allowed Brens, Mortars and Wirelessmen to use their sangars except for heavy stonking, as I was afraid with only 10 yards between us and the crest, we might easily be rushed if the men had their heads down. When I went back up, things were about the same although we were getting thin on the ground. All the time the tempo was increasing. The mortaring was heavier etc. By now we were all using sangars.

Round about 3.30, we had the worst blow of all. The pill box was suddenly blasted to pieces by an SP gun and every time we poked over the crest the same thing happened. This made us very blind and the stonk we called for was not much help. Brian Rudd arrived at this stage with his platoon (2 Company) and the last I saw before leaving was Krauts on the crest and everyone fighting like hell. Sgt. Bailey and three or four Guardsmen suddenly got up and charged them, which seemed to clear a few of them. I went to David Toler and told him our position – rather incoherently, I am afraid, as I had taken some blast from our 25 pounders, and he got ready to deal with it if it got worse. I then met Hugo, badly wounded in the head. I sent him back on an ambulance jeep and would have returned to Brian but for David and Elston who had me in their clutches. It was a fearful position for Brian because it was much more than one officer could deal with – especially one who had only been there a few minutes. Five minutes talk to him and the CSM would have helped him a lot, but it was not to be. I spoke to him on the wireless and he said he had everything in hand. When I knew I was definitely going back, I am afraid I collapsed like a pricked balloon and the disappointment of leaving men, without an officer, who had fought so splendidly, was one of the bitterest of my life – hence my pitiful condition when you saw me – I feel very bad about this, especially as I vaguely remember the Brigadier being there.

Out of it all I should say we had a small attack at night and one fairly big one in the morning (when No. 3 moved a bit) and a bigger one in the afternoon. All the time there was fighting from the moment we reached the top, but it was mainly individuals in small groups. You will probably know definitely by now, but I believe we accounted for a good many Germans – chiefly with our Brens.

As I tried to tell you before I left, our main trouble was fatigue – we were a very tired company before the attack started and then the baking sun on the scorching rocks was wearing us down the whole time. We had no food and little water until Brian came up, and, but for those things, I am sure we were as safe as houses. I need not say how the men behaved.'

Letter to my Grandmother from Guy Charteris

Bishopstone,
Bridge-Sollars,
Hereford.
7.VI.44

Dear Mrs Neilson,
From the enclosed you will see that I am carrying out my son's instructions. I had the bulk of his letter typed hastily and it will save me trouble if I send you a copy. Since the coming of the awful telegram I had had no details so it was a great relief to hear first from my son. I expect you too had the good news direct. Perhaps I should have left out 'out in a fortnight or so' but let's hope the war in Italy will be over by then.

Yours sincerely,

Guy Charteris

Tuesday May 30

How hot it is in this brown tent with the sides up and walls of ripening corn growing all round. My ear and head wounds yielded some grenade casing last night and are less rather than more comfortable for having done so. However, the Lord for us wrought marvellously and in one fierce day's fighting we declared in deed and fact 'nemo me impune lacessit'. There is so much to say, pages and pages worth, but the last weeks I have lived outside myself and never once was able to feel the joy of essences, so that now I can think of little to say....

Meanwhile find Andrew Neilson's mother address and tell her that the company of men he trained for two years so excellently, he led in action no less well. He continued to command the company for six hours after he was wounded and was at all times energetic and resolute, even when he became light-headed from loss of blood, and walked round from trench to trench to see the men, with a stretcher bearer holding horizontal his tourniquetted arm; like an eighteenth century lord and lady daintily footing it in to dinner they were.

I almost certainly killed my German – fifteen foot: a short aimed burst from the shoulder—- you would not have been able to complain 'do take them in the head—- that's no good for eating'—because only his head was showing. The dust boiled in the correct place, but before I could check up a stick grenade wheeled into the sky from another quarter and I received a box on the ear which felled me to my knees. Beneath me I saw the grey dust and stone and coarse grass suddenly resplendent with a great spattering of brilliant blood. That dust and blood had been a familiar cocktail since dawn, and I was completely unhorrified.

As to the men of the company—Andrew and I, now in neighbouring beds, this afternoon tried to decide which of them deserved decorations. But no sooner did we pick on one when we would say: 'But what about so-and-so and so-and-so—till we had considered the names of about 50% of the company. A hopeless job: they were all excellent.

If the wound goes septic, I will have to have a grafting operation – there is a sizeable hole through my ear and a groove in my ear. 'A little louder, please. That ear's deaf y'know. German grenade in '44'. The walnut complexion is coming on—soon all I'll need to do is shave the back of my neck and learn the trick of clearing my throat like an anchor chain running out.

Andrew has a piece of grenade in the arm and will be out in a fortnight or so. 78 Murray House, Vendon Street, Buckingham Gate. His mother's address. Please write.

So much love to you.   Hugo

*A letter from Andrew Neilson to his mother whilst he was on sick leave in Rome,
1944*

Rome, June 21st.

My dear Mother,

Since leaving hospital I have hardly had a moment to myself so consequently I
have neglected correspondence. Fortunately, I have been occupied not in the
dangerous pursuits of war but of pleasure. I was in hospital for only 10 days,
most of which time I spent with Tim; then Hugo Charteris and myself were
discharged together with a recommendation for 14 days' sick leave. We returned
to the battalion and went straight on leave. We helped ourselves to a car from a
Fascist and then came here, where we have secured a flat in the most fashionable
quarter of Rome. With plenty of food, scrounged from the well-supplied
Americans, Rome was at our feet. We have been entertained royally. Our best
friends are a circle of Swiss, all of whom are absolutely charming and very
intellectual and artistic. The big Italian families – Colonna's, Torlonia's,
Borghese's, etc. live on a scale unsurpassed by any royalty in the world, but apart
from that they lack dignity and present a poor aspect of such a humiliated
nation.

When I was in hospital two parcels from you were sent on to me – both intact!
– containing candles, Milton, Shakespeare, Macaulay, Golden Treasury,
dictionaries, Being Met Together (a very good novel indeed) and probably
some other books I can't remember. Thank you very much, I am enjoying
them a lot.

Rome is a wonderful city, very open, large buildings and plenty of trees and
flowers. The streets crowded with attractive well-dressed women. The only
shortage at all is food and there is an ample Black Market for that. The War has
left Rome almost untouched. Unfortunately the hordes of Americans have put
the prices up beyond our means already. We called one day at the Convent where
the Abbot and monks of Monte Cassino are now staying; the Abbot was very
bitter about the bombing and was hardly polite to us. He insisted that there were
no Germans in the Monastery before the bombing I think he thought we had
called in some official capacity and was very disappointed when we told him we
had called unofficially!

Another day we went to one of the public audiences of the Pope; it was a
very impressive ceremony and he spoke in reasonable English. A friend of ours
in the Swiss Guard showed us round parts of the Vatican. Everything and
everyone here is full of interest. We have met some of the 2,000 escaped
Prisoners of War who have been in hiding in Rome for six months or more and
we heard of their organisations. Fascinating stories they have.

On Friday we return to the battalion and what awaits us there I don't know. I
don't even know where they are!

Give my love to everyone and I hope you are all all right. Tell the girls I will
write to them when I have time, but at the moment I have none. The Invasion

seems a success and I hope Churchill is right when he says the War may be over by the Autumn. I haven't had any letters for a month; they will all be waiting for me, I hope.

With love, Andrew.

CHAPTER 4

From Arce to Perugia and
Monte Pacciano

As a result of the action at Monte Piccolo, 'S' Company was desperately short of officers. Captain Neilson and Lieutenant Charteris were wounded and in hospital and Lieutenant Bridgeman had been killed. CSM Brown had consolidated the Company's positions after the enemy had made no further attempts to counter-attack. Lieutenant J.S. Wilson, who had been on leave hiked back when he heard the news. Lieutenants J.E. Baxter and the Hon. C.D. Dalrymple were quickly sent up from IRTD to take over platoons and Major Cuthbert resumed command of the Company. 'S' Company had time to take stock at this moment of the lessons learnt from this, their first major action. They had time to reorganise and take care of casualties and, at the same time, arrange for a change in dress from battledress to something cooler and more effective for the Summer months. Khaki drill, used in North Africa, was too bright a colour for use in the green and brown hills of Umbria. They chose khaki shirts and dark green denim trousers, covered by para-type smocks – this combination proved to be very efficient.

On 1 June, 2nd Battalion Coldstream Guards set off up Route 6 and after a night at Ceprano, they turned north into the hills, advancing through Frosinone, Alatri and Fuomone until they reached Lake Canterno where they spent two days at rest, bathing in the lake. 'S' Company and 2nd Battalion Coldstream Guards continued a slow advance behind the Arno, via Fiuggi and Genazzano (6 June) to bivouac only six miles from Rome, which they could just catch a glimpse of in the setting sun. 1st Guards Brigade were at this point directed up the Tiber towards Terni, some 50 miles to the North. The Grenadiers, advancing as the vanguard, came across an enemy rearguard at Monterotondo, through which they forced their way, as the Coldstream relaxed by the fast-flowing Tiber. Captain Neilson and Lieutenant Charteris appeared from hospital whilst here and were sent on 14 days' sick leave. On 9 June, the Coldstream took the lead again and bumped along behind the tanks of 17/21 Lancers, until they were held up by a blown up bridge over the River Farfa, a tributary of the Tiber. Two miles further, the enemy had put together a strong position where the Tiber ran through a narrow defile under M. Sabini. This was quite clearly a task for infantry. At dusk 'S' Company was part of the advance to Poggio Mirteto Station and took the hill on the right of the gorge, whilst 4 Company, under Captain Toler, took the left, with only a little opposition from shelling. This was the end to the problems at Farfa crossing, and later that night the Grenadier and Welsh Guards passed through.

10 June was a devastating day for 2nd Battalion Coldstream Guards. Enemy shelling was becoming intense and just as it was getting dark a salvo hit Battalion Headquarters at Poggio Mirteto, wounding the Commanding Officer, Colonel Hugh Norman, his adjutant, Capt. Chaplin, and the Support Company Commander, Major Windsor-Clive. Major Alderson was killed in a scout car and a total of five other ranks were killed. Among those killed was CQMS A. McDade of 'S' Company who had provided sterling support with re-supply at Cassino. CQMS J. McLay joined the company in his place. A night attack that night by the Grenadiers and Welsh Guards on either flank caused the enemy to withdraw. Major R.E.J.C.M. Coates came forward and assumed command of the Battalion.

The successful outcome of this brief hold up meant that the Battalion could advance behind the tanks for eight days without hindrance. The route, through some of the best Italian countryside took them through Narni and Todi. Having covered some 60 miles in seven days, on 18 June they came up to a point four miles short of Perugia, where the Grenadiers were holding positions. Patrols were ordered with 'S' Company being given the task of entering the town.

Two patrols sent in from different sides were fired on and were unable to enter the town, having only reached the suburbs. The Grenadiers were counter-attacked on 19 June, with heavy shelling in dreadful rain. After a day of unpleasant conditions, the railway station fell to forward Coldstream companies at dawn on 20 June. Further patrols found the town free of Germans.

Again the enemy had slipped away under cover of darkness, allowing the Coldstream with 'S' Company in the lead to move through to regain contact with the enemy to the north of the town. About two miles north stood the 2000ft. feature of Monte Pacciano, which dominated the northern aspects. It was here that 'S' Company fought a brief engagement by night just short of the summit. They remained here for the next two days under heavy shellfire, until relieved by 2 Company on 22 June. After four further days of patrolling to probe the enemy positions, it was decided to clear the mountain completely with an attack involving all three Battalions (25 June). This night attack started in the early hours and was completely successful – 'S' Company on this occasion was held in reserve. Patrols later found the enemy in positions

Monte Pacciano from San Marco, near Perugia 2003

around Civitella, some five miles to the north. 'S' Company had by this time been withdrawn into Perugia town.

On 1 July, the Coldstream were relieved and spent a memorable night in Perugia, later moving down to the south of Lake Trasimene to a rest area in the hills at Castiglioni Fosco. Here they rested and sorted themselves out in glorious sunshine.

Appendix 'B' to War Diary June 1944
The Battle for Pacciano
German skill and the difficulties of the ground caused confusion during the battle and it frequently happened that the companies had little information on one another's movements, especially at night. The following account may help to clarify the course of the battle and the controlling factors.

The object of the attack was to clear the enemy OPs from the crest of the hill from which Perugia and the exits from the town were under observation. All the information about the enemy positions was gained by our patrols and those of the Derby Yeomanry. Sangars had been reported on the crest facing

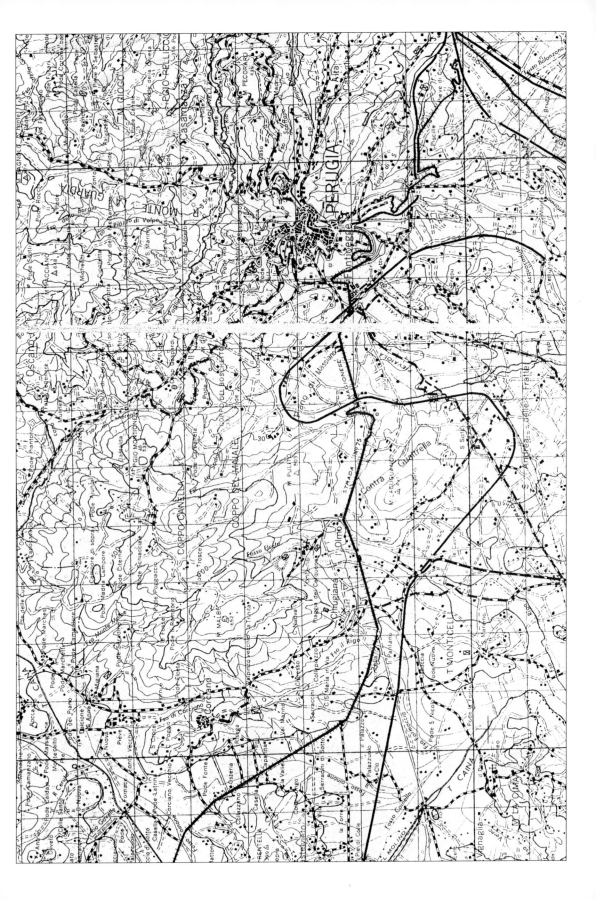

west and Sgt. Marshall, with the three Guardsmen from No. 3 Company's very gallant daylight patrol, located machine guns in the wooded gully. This was later confirmed by Lieutenant Dalrymple's 'S' Company patrol.

The plan of attack was for No. 2 Company and 'S' Company to remain in their present positions acting as firm bases and reserves if necessary. No. 4 Company was to move up to the White House at dusk and from there to assault the top of the hill. No. 3 Company, from its forming up place at Haystack Farm, had to sweep along the right hand side of the wooded gully and dig in on the left of No. 4. It was hoped that in the darkness and close cover of the gully they could destroy the known enemy machine gun posts.

Here is a sequence of the events:-

0900 hrs.   2, 3 and 4 Companies leave for FUP

0115 hrs.   Considerable amount of Spandau fire coming from gully.

0150 hrs.   Major Palmer reports that 4 machine guns are firing from his objective and that plans are being made for the final assault.

0210 hrs.   Captain Chichester rings up from No. 2 Coy. HQ to report that 3 Company ran into 6 Spandaus at very close range and that they have suffered casualties. The Commanding Officer orders 3 Company to take the best defensive position they can find in their area.

0230 hrs.   Major Palmer reports over his 18 Set that one of his platoons is on its objective, the Welsh Guards report that they are very close to their objective on the left of the gully.

0255 hrs.   The Commanding Officer orders No. 2 Company to move two platoons to take up a position on the ridge between 3 and 4 Companies overlooking the gully.

0325 hrs.   2 Company leave their old position.

At first light all companies are dug in and in position and no enemy is to be seen.

It is not difficult to see the task which each company undertook and the effect it had on the battle.

'S' Coy., by originally establishing themselves less than 500 yds from the top of Pacciano, gave the other companies the opportunity of getting FUPs very close to their objectives.

No. 3 Company, by engaging the machine guns in the wooded gully, enabled the Welsh Guards and No. 2 Company to get to their objectives without difficulty. No. 4 Company, by reaching the top of the crest and overlooking the Germans in the gully, made it impossible for them to remain there. No. 2. Company managed to fill the gap between 3 and 4 Companies, completing their advance and digging in in the hour which remained before daylight. When the ground was examined in daylight the bodies of one German Officer and three German other ranks were found left behind by the Germans. It is estimated that the enemy had a weak company on the feature, armed with at least 12 machine guns, which is not particularly weak opposition for a two Company attack.

WARTIME MEMORIES by the Hon. C.D. Dalrymple

On 30 May 1944 I was at the Infantry Reinforcement Training Depot at Rotondi – not far from Benerento. I had been there for three months since the 2nd Battalion Scots Guards had been sent home and had left behind all those who had not served overseas for very long. I had only done three months but it had included the follow up after the crossing of the River Gariglioni, near its mouth, in January. I had therefore seen something of the reality of war – if only for a short time. It had cost the lives of our Commanding Officer, and four other officers with an equivalent proportion of Guardsmen.

I cannot pretend that the news that I was to replace Humphrey Bridgeman, who had been killed, was received without a measure of apprehension. I had wanted to get away from the IRTD since the day I arrived but the news from the Cassino area had been grim in the extreme and there seemed to be little prospect of the future being any less so. Humphrey was the second platoon commander to be killed in 'S' Company in that area.

The following day, 31 May 1944, I left Rotondi with a small draft of men for 'S' Company and the 2nd Battalion Coldstream Guards. We drove via Capua to Cassino which took a long time on densly crowded roads. The remains of the town, which we semi-bypassed on a bulldozered track, was a ghastly sight; it was reduced to an area of complete rubble. We found our destination about fifteen miles north along Route 6 at a place called Castelione. As for much of the summer, we were camped out in bivouac tents, which are extremely pleasant in Italy at that time of year.

I was to remain with that Company till it returned to Pirbright, two and a half years later in 1947.

The next day we continued our advance. 6th Armoured Division, of which 1st Guards Brigade formed part, was on a comparatively narrow front much congested by the lack of roads and the mountainous country, which now began to open out. We travelled in Troop Carrying Vehicles, which were 4x4 Bedfords with incredibly uncomfortable seats. Each was supposed to hold a platoon of 28 men, which was manifestly impossible, particularly with the kit and weapons they had to carry. As an officer, I usually had an excuse to lead the way in the fifteen hundredweight truck, until by magic, the era of the jeep introduced sanity into the transport scene.

Our halting progress took us through Arce (suitably re-named by the Guardsmen), and across the River Lire on a Bailey Bridge at Ceprano. Eventually we parked in a field to await our next turn in the order of march.

Although we had left behind the formidable range of mountains which the Germans had used for their Gustav Line, the more open country still provided them with a series of minor obstacles, which they were able to fortify in various ways. First they blew up every bridge and most of the significant culverts, which crossed every road. In addition these were usually sown with mines which had to be cleared before the chasm could be bull-dozed in. The result was often casualties to the sappers, followed by some very steep and awkward bits of track, and these were vulnerable to occasional thunder showers. In Italy they can be sensational and our by-passes invariably washed away.

The roads themselves were totally different from what they are today. Apart from a few main ones – such as Route 6 from Cassino to Rome, they were mostly narrow and untarred. Clouds of very fine dust rose behind every vehicle and we proceeded in a dense cloud which penetrated everything. In forward areas great care had to be taken not to stir it up as it invariably attracted shell fire if in range of our enemy.

We remained in this nice peaceful field until suddenly required to move at 0130 hrs on 3 June '44. This unsocial start took the Battalion through Frosinone to a point on the road towards Alatri. The roadside continued to be lined with the wreckage of German equipment, which had fallen victim to the Air Forces. This included a number of their newer tanks, which we had been hearing so much about. But mines were always a worry on these moves because they had been laid in all sorts of places along these roads where vehicles might be expected to turn off or park. Swept areas were marked with notices and white tape but unfortunately that was not always enough.

On 4 June '44 we heard that General Mark Clark and his 88th Division of Blue Devils had got to Rome a few miles to the west of us. Strategically it seemed less important to us than apparently it was to him for publicity reasons.

At 0615 on 5 June we moved again. We passed through Alatri to

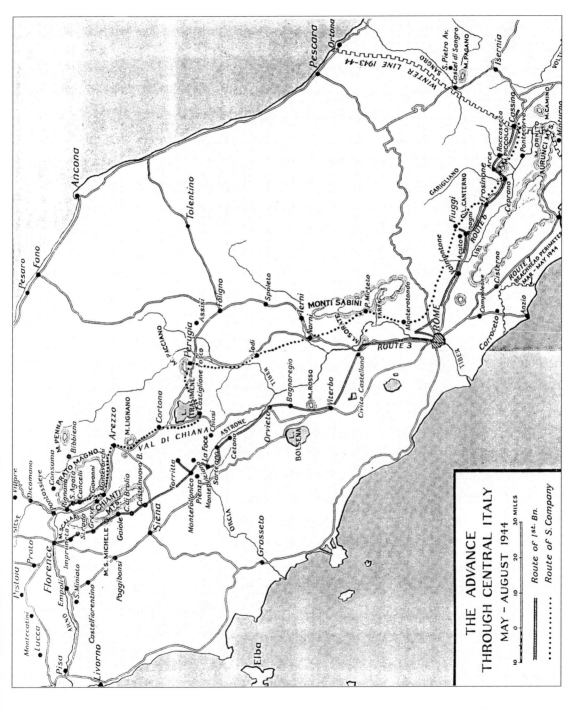

THE ADVANCE
THROUGH CENTRAL ITALY
MAY – AUGUST 1944

————— Route of 1st. Bn.
▬▬▬▬▬ Route of S. Company
················ Route of S. Company

Trivigliano, two small and attractive towns, perched characteristically on hill tops. The fifteen mile journey took three hours and might have been more pleasant on foot. Burnt out German transport continued to litter the verges encouraging us, wrongly, to believe that the enemy was defeated.

Late in the evening, the Battalion received orders to prepare for twenty four hours on wheels and that our first destination was to be Terni. I, on the other hand, was detailed to make a very early start and go back to IRTD and bring up another draft of men. I set off at 0500 hrs on 6 June and drove back to Rotondi in a TCV. The following morning my draft included some Grenadiers and Welsh guardsmen. I decided that it might be more fun and not much longer to go north along the coast road rather than Route 6 by Cassino, which I knew to be heavily over-crowded. We crossed the Gariglione near Pontefiume, where I had been in January. We stopped for a brew up near Anzio and then continued into Rome where we found it convenient to halt again in the Piazza Veneziana by the Victor Emmanuel monument. It was an amazing spectacle to watch an unbroken stream of American lorries driving through the Square where Mussolini used to deliver his most important speeches. Despite this diversion, I succeeded in finding the Battalion on the Terni road (via Salernia) before anything dramatic had happened and I was rather surprised that they had not got further on.

Perhaps it should be reported that, as the Division was on quite a narrow front and further constricted by the lack of roads, Battalions took it in turns to lead and likewise companies within them. The result was a great deal of lingering in a succession of concentration areas and a good deal of stress from the certain knowledge that trouble lay ahead and that we could be called upon for harder things at any time.

One such event came about on 10 June. After only a short move the Battalion came in for long range shelling with disasterous results. They landed on Headquarter Company where Captain Dick Alderson and our quartermaster sergeant, McDade, were killed. The Commanding Officer, Lt-Colonel Hugh Norman and his adjutant, Dick Chaplin, were badly wounded and never returned to us. Bob Windsor Clive was also wounded but able to come back before too long.

From 10 to 18 June there were a series of moves at inconvenient hours of the day or night and by then we reached San Martino, about six miles south of Perugia. Then things changed. Heavy rain converted our clouds of dust into a slimey mud and our comfortable camping turned into a competition to get inside any building with a roof on it. This of course resulted in groups of men where, within reach of shell fire, dispersal was a measure of protection.

During the night of 18 June the company remained at San Martino. I was told to take out a patrol and try to establish contact and the whereabouts of the Germans on our line of advance. I followed David Toler's company for much of the night along the railway line which skirts the south side of Perugia and leads through a short tunnel to the station. As dawn began to break, David decided, correctly, to stop and dig in just short of the tunnel. I, perhaps unwisely, chose to go through it as I could vaguely see the other end. When I got there I found that it was indeed still occupied by the Germans, who presumably thought it safe and dry. I returned to report their whereabouts and was perhaps lucky to do so unscathed.

Two other things happened that night. Gerald Lascelles, now Lord Harewood, was sent out on a similar mission by the Grenadiers; he ended up in Colditz. Our Quartermaster Sergeant, bringing up rations, overshot San Martino and similarly went into the bag. No doubt the enemy enjoyed our ration of stewed meat and vegetables.

On 19 June '44 the company advanced on foot through David Toler's position onto the next small hill. It was still raining and another very uncomfortable night was suffered. No one seemed to know what had happened to the Quartermaster and we got no food.

On 20 June the company moved twice during the day: the second time taking us up into the north west corner of Perugia, whence it was possible to see a long way over the country to the North. The principal feature in that direction lay across a deep valley and was called Monte Pacciano, 648 metres high and about 3 km distant from our chosen viewpoint on the city walls. 'S' Company was ordered to advance up this feature and so we had a company order group at our vantage point. Certain intermediate features were identified and each platoon was to advance to one of them and the rest of the company to pass through. My turn with No. 9 Platoon (Sergeant Copeland) was to take over from Sgt. Young's platoon about three quarters of the way up and continue to the top.

As the evening light failed, we made our way out of the town and into the intervening valley. There we met a German Corporal who said that he wished to surrender. After a few unsuccessful questions about the whereabouts of his friends, we told him to continue into Perugia and give himself up there.

In darkness we proceeded with extreme caution and making every effort to achieve complete silence. It is surprisingly difficult for a hundred men to do this when carrying full equipment, weapons and picks and shovels. It was a dark, starlit night and, as was the custom, some searchlights in the rear areas playing on clouds, gave a measure of artificial moonlight. Everyone knew that

45

at some point we would find opposition lying out and waiting for us.

When we were about four hundred yards from the top the leading section lay down. From a few yards back, I crawled forward and whispered to the Section Commander who replied that he had heard movement by some trees – perhaps thirty yards ahead on a slight ridge: better described as a false summit of the top. Two men rose to their feet on this skyline and I fired my Tommy gun at each in turn. The section then also let fly and the figures disappeared over the ridge. We got up and advanced to the line of trees when a spandau started to fire at us and its muzzle flashes were visible we all responded. Sadly, one man was killed in this exchange.

Having established where our enemy was, it was extremely difficult in the dark to know how we could attack. Confusion on such occasions usually resulted in casualties and very uncertain results. It was therefore decided to 'dig in' on our reverse slope. A decision which seemed reasonable by virtue of the fact that neither our company wireless set nor that of our gunner forward observation officer were in touch with their base stations and after our long slow climb, we believed that we were even further out in front of the Battalion than was actually the case.

On 21 June '44 the later hours of the night were spent digging slit trenches to form an 'all round' defensive position. The ground was very hard and there was little earth cover over rock below. The sun rose in the general direction of Assisi and there was a wonderful view over the ancient city of Perugia and down the Tiber valley but everyone was far too tired to appreciate things like that.

During the day, the rest of the Battalion closed up on us with David Toler's company just below and behind us. No doubt this movement was seen because a period of heavy shelling ensued. Luckily these skimmed low over our heads, narrowly clearing the line of trees ahead but there was one airburst and we had another man killed. For Toler's company, however, things were far worse as they had sixteen casualties including one platoon commander, Peter Gale, killed.

On 22 June '44 'S' Company remained in the same position after another night and during a very hot shadeless day. During the early night, No. 2 Company took over the position and we retired to reserve about half a mile back. Andrew Neilson and Hugo Charteris rejoined the company on 24 June and a battalion attack reached the top of Monte Pacciano on 27 June at the further cost of 5 men killed and 20 wounded. During this period one officer was taken prisoner on patrol.

The action at Perugia was a small affair in the general context of the advance up Italy. I have described our share in some detail as I think it was characteristic of many such others which were required to clear the minor defensive positions used by the Germans to delay our progress. That progress was much slower and more laborious than might have been expected and, as described, resulted in a steady drain of casualties.

CHAPTER 5

Monte Lignano
14–16 July 1944

Those who went for Arezzo were soon held up by strong enemy positions on the dominating heights of Monte Lignano, which rose to almost 3,000 ft. five miles to the south of the town. From these positions the enemy were able to command the whole of the wide Chiana valley to the south and west and to observe and shell any plumes of dust, without which movement was almost impossible, on the white roads below them. Only infantry could attack such a position and the task was allotted to the 2nd New Zealand Division and to the First Guards Brigade.

This news reached the Battalion on 5 July and they at once began to move forward via Borghetto, on the shores of Lake Trasimene, and on to Camucia. At this stage Major Cuthbert left the Company to take over the Scots Guards element at the IRTD, taking with him Lieutenant Baxter, and Captain Neilson assumed command. Next followed a week of intense preparation for the attack, during which every section commander was shown the objective, a razor backed ridge sprinkled with farm houses, from a ground O.P. Company and Platoon Commanders pored over air photographs, whilst the Guardsmen were briefed on a sand model which showed as near as possible every contour of the ground over which they were to fight.

A captured German operation order showed that the 15th Panzer Grenadier Division were holding the line in front of Arrezo and that Monte Lignano itself, which was to be the New Zealanders' objective, was held in some strength; whilst no one had any illusions that the North Western slopes, including the l'Olmo Pass, for which First Guards Brigade were responsible, were any less strongly held. The Coldstream were to attack through the Grenadiers and on the night of 14 July they moved up to the foot of the mountain and lay down on the hillside to wait for the word to advance. Nothing was heard until five o'clock next morning and it was already getting light as the companies roused themselves and began to climb the hill. No. 4 Company went first, with 'S' behind them, and they were almost up to the Grenadier positions when the enemy pounded the area with mortar bombs and threw in a determined counter attack which forced the Grenadiers back. All was confused for quite a time but with Coldstream support, the Grenadiers were able to regain their positions and No. 4 Company passed through to take its own objective.

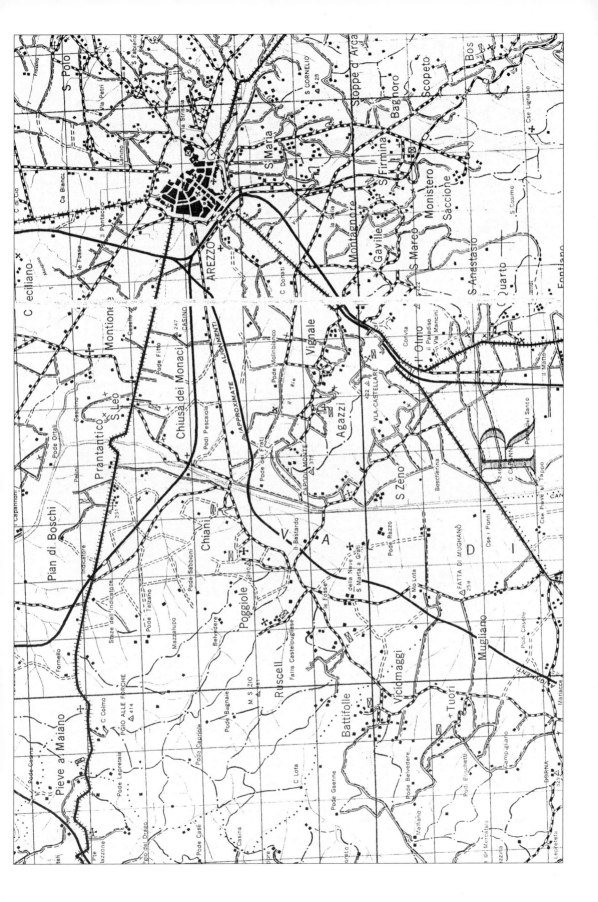

'S' Company were given the signal to advance soon after midday and hardly had they left No. 4 Company's area than Captain Neilson stepped on a schu mine which wounded him so severely that he died on the following day. Lieutenant Charteris at once took over command and led the Company on through heavy machine fire to attack the first of their three objectives, Point 501. 'It was the hardest attack that 'S' Company had ever done', records the Coldstream History. 'The Germans fought stubbornly with every weapon they could command, but the Scots Guardsmen wormed their way up the hill and cleared the near slope of it with grenade and bayonet. Beyond that they could not go: Lieutenant Charteris was badly wounded. Company Sergeant Major Brown, the hero of Monte Piccolo, was killed and the Company (now commanded by Lieutenant Wilson, its only surviving officer) could only hang on to its gains while the enemy remained on the forward slope.' Lance-Sergeant Jones of Monte Piccolo fame was also killed, as were five others, whilst 10 more were wounded in the furious fighting which developed on the hill-top. In such circumstances are heroes made and Lance Sergeant McPhail,

Track up to the objective on Monte Lignano 2003

commanding the leading section in the assault, was such a one. Nearing the crest he found his way dominated by a strongly reinforced German dugout from which was coming a hail of heavy Spandau fire. Calling for his section PIAT he ran with it out into the open and fired two bombs at a distance of only twenty yards, effectively silencing the strong point and allowing his men to capture the position. Later in the battle, after the officer casualties had occurred he took over command of his platoon. Sergeant Young, the Platoon Sergeant of No. 8 Platoon when the battle started, did much the same, taking over from the Company Sergeant Major as soon as he had been killed and later from Lieutenant Charteris. At one moment, when the shelling was particularly heavy, he volunteered to crawl over the crest to direct our own gunfire and whilst so doing a piece of shell fragment tore the gas cape from off his back. For their part in the battle for Monte Lignano, Sergeant W.G. Young was awarded the Distinguished Conduct Medal and Lance Sergeant McPhail the Military Medal.

For some hours Battalion Headquarters had no news at all of 'S' Company,

Area of S Anastasio on Monte Lignano near S Company's objective 2003

since the Company signallers were all casualties and so also was Lieutenant Charteris who had worked the wireless under similar circumstances on Monte Piccolo. However, as soon as Colonel Coates heard of their situation and of their casualties, he at once sent up No. 2 Company to their assistance. But by the time they arrived on the hill top they found Point 501 clear of the enemy and patrols which went out during the night confirmed that the enemy had gone. Next morning the supporting tanks drove through the l'Olmo Pass and into Arezzo and the weary infantry descended the slopes to the music of pealing bells.

Extract from the diary of Major the Hon. Colin Dalrymple

Thursday 13 July 44
No move. Full and elaborate plans have been made for a brigade attack on the N.W. slopes of Lignano which blocks the road to Arezzo. It only remains for the convenient time to arrive for the whole thing to start and that depends on a New Zealand brigade, which has come up on our right.

P.S. During the afternoon I met Andrew Neilson walking across the farmyard round which we were encamped. He was carrying a message form and looked completely shattered. 'I have just heard that my mother has been killed by a bomb in the Guards' Chapel' he said.

Friday 14 July 44
After a quiet day, the battalion moved late in the evening. There seems every reason to expect unpleasantness during the next day or two. I stayed at 'A' Echelon.

Saturday 15 July 44
During the morning the news from the battalion was quite good but later a message came in that Andrew Neilson was wounded and that I was to go up to the company. Further enquiries revealed that he had trodden on a schu mine which had blown off one foot and damaged the other. All this happened on a path along which several hundred people had already passed.

When I reached Bn.HQ, which was near the main road at the foot of the mountain, I heard that Hugo Charteris had also been wounded. Just after I got inside the house where the HQ was functioning, a number of large shells landed round it, one actually hit the side but fortunately did not penetrate. After getting hold of a guide, I set off up the hill which was very steep, it was very hot, rather alarming and generally most unpleasant. All the way I met wounded men coming down, at one place there were three dead Germans, which I was thoroughly pleased to see. Hugo was being brought down on a stretcher looking white and exhausted but talking quite normally and obviously not in a serious condition. I stopped for a time at Fwd.BnHQ and then went on to the Company which was in a good position on a little hill with a bare top and thick trees round most of the sides. Company Sergeant Major Brown had been killed by a shell, and four others. A dozen had been wounded and two of them were still lying waiting to be carried away, but owing to distance and the time taken to get earlier cases to the RAP, we were without stretchers and they were too bad to move without. I made the hell of a fuss on the wireless and eventually got results.

No shells arrived in our area after I got there. No.2 Company Coldstream Guards went forward about midnight onto the next hill without meeting opposition and then the Welsh Guards attacked a stage further. They used an enormous amount of artillery, which caused them four casualties and proved to be rather wasteful as the huns had already gone.

Sunday 16 July 44

So far as we were concerned, the night was quiet enough but rather chilly. I got separated from my pack and was only dressed in a sweat shirt and trousers with a camouflage smock over the top.

We expected the huns to fire off all spare ammunition and depart as the place could hold no further interest for them once we were on all the high points and could see right beyond Arezzo to the River Arno. To my relief, they merely went away so we spent the morning examining their positions and wondering why they had left no corpses for it seems certain that they must have had plenty of casualties. This is a perpetual mystery for there never seems to be an adequate number of German graves. The armoured brigade passed Arezzo and crossed the Arno on bridges which had not been blown, as the engineer responsible was still waiting for some of his own people. We buried our own dead, cleaned up all the equipment which is always lying about on such occasions and walked down to the main road. On the way we met Brig. Charles Heyden who told us that Andrew had died in the early morning. We settled down in a field for the night. The prospect of the events of the last 48 hours being frequently repeated makes me feel exhausted, depressed and thoroughly miserable.

P.S. During the morning, the Commanding Officer, Col. Bob Coates, came up to our position with our Roman Catholic Padre, Father George Forbes, MC. We buried Company Sergeant Major Brown and our other four dead in the usual sad little field service.

Monday 17 July 44
A busy day trying to organize the Company and arrange for reinforcements. Col. Bob Coates says that he wants me to command the company and will try to get another captain. However, I doubt if this will be approved elsewhere as there is no shortage of captains senior to myself and several available majors. It would be nice to have control of the jeep all the same.

Tuesday 18 July 44
No move. Further labours with the question of promotion and the need to strike a tactful balance between the qualifications of efficiency and seniority. The battle of Monte Lignano has had a good press with us and obviously produced good results but so far as I am concerned the loss of Andrew and CSM Brown in one day fully outweighs anything else.

A letter received by Andrew Neilson (his nickname was Jock) just before the battle of Monte Lignano. Mrs Lisa Puckle was a great friend of his mother

78 Park Mansions,
Knightsbridge
London, S.W.1.

KEN 4232   23 June 1944

My dear Jock,

It is so difficult to write because whatever I can say will be completely inadequate to give you what I really feel about the terrible tragedy, which has overwhelmed you personally and in general all regiments of Guards; we are all so close to it here and are still being afflicted day and night by their rockets and even thus the sense of loss in unbelievable, while with you, it will be far worse, and the shock dreadful.

There is one thing I am sure of and that is that your dear Mother was as proud of you and your work, and felt so close to all your life when she was in that lovely chapel (she told me that herself) that she would have chosen her passing over to take place where it did, and as it did, rather than anywhere else, and I am so glad to feel how delighted she was over your last letter and its good news, but it is owing to the fact that she was such a devoted and loving mother that a blank will be left in your life, which makes me able to think of your Mother's kindness to me, quite unconscious on her part and therefore doubly appreciated, in those dreary hard days I spent in Cheltenham while Sheila was at College, and her subsequent friendship and the good jaunts we had together will always be a very dear memory in my life and a very grateful one, and I shall miss her terribly.

I do hope your arm is quite fit now, and things are otherwise going well with you? Remember don't scruple to call on me if you want anything done in town and if I can be of any use at any time. Take care of yourself. We go along and have reverted, more or less, to the atmosphere of the Blitz days and particularly nights, which is more trying after nearly five years than after one.

Father sends his best wishes and deepest sympathy. With much love and the most heartfelt sympathy.

Yours always, Lisa Puckle.

This was probably the last letter from Andrew Neilson to his sister, my mother

Capt. A.S. Neilson,
'S' Coy 2CG CMF,
8 July 1944
My dear Margaret,
As you can well imagine I was very shocked and very upset to hear of our Mother's death. I had been in Rome for a fortnight's leave after hospital; I returned to the battalion on the Friday night and the next day I went in to the line. About four days later I came out for one and a half days and we were eating luncheon in a lovely villa we had taken over in the town when I was brought a letter from Mrs Puckle. The conversation was about the bomb in the Chapel and as I read the letter (which took it for granted I knew all about it) I realised what Mrs P was saying. That was the first I heard of it. The next day I had a cable from Anne who had seen it in the Times. That evening I went in again and when the battalion came out a few days later the air letters from you and Mary were waiting for me, also one from Anne and Bogey (both very sweet and sympathic). Since then I have had your cable and a further air letter from you; I have also heard from Archie Pearson, and Col. Archie. The hole it leaves in one's life is very big – and in my case the hole in the life I look back on and look forward to – and I felt very distressed and apathetic even though I am now used to death on the grand scale. My depression was brought to its lowest possible ebb by hearing the following day that Bill Vestey and the Commanding Officer of 1st Battalion Scots Guards were killed together. Poor Pamela! One begins to wonder how and when it will all end and whether, after all, it was worth all the sacrifice. Thank God Tim has gone off to Palestine as ADC to some General. He at least should be safe.

Fortunately I haven't had much time to sit about and think – thus the time I have taken to write, we are pushing on, as you know, and we hope soon for a long rest, as everyone is very tired. I am now commanding the company as we got rid of David Cuthbert by all passing a no-confidence vote, whether I shall be confirmed in this or not I don't know. But it means at the moment that I can't possibly get home. If the situation changes, I will certainly try to arrange it somehow.

You and Mary must have had a dreadful time and I feel deeply sorry for you

55

both. I think we will all realise now what a wonderful Mother she was – especially me, who gave so little in return. But it is no good any of us blaming ourselves for no one is to blame for such a tragedy except the perpetrator himself. I am still getting letters from her, all of which talk either of just having gone to a service there or of just going to one. They are horrible reminders. As far any settling has to be done, I agree it is best left until we all meet again, but if there is anything of immediate importance I am sure Thompson's advice is valuable.

I am sorry to write in pencil but in these circumstances ink is not practicable. I hope you are all well – I will write to Mary soon. I am completely recovered but very tired again and looking forward to a long rest. Give my love to all, write when you can and don't upset yourself with Mary.

All love, Andrew.

CHAPTER 6

Advance to Gothic Line

Despite the presence of 'S' Company in the Second Coldstream, there was still a grave shortage of reinforcements to fill the other three Rifle Companies; a problem in which the Eighth Army Commander, Lieutenant General Sir Oliver Leese, took considerable interest. At the same time the Scots Guards Company at the IRTD had seldom less than four hundred men on its rolls and thus, just as 'S' Company had been conceived, so it was planned to form a second company of Scots Guardsmen under Captain R.G. Rowe to be attached to the Battalion. Despite the fact that this Company actually formed and trained together for several weeks under the name of 'X' Company and Colonel Coates wrote a letter to his Regimental Headquarters in London on 19 July saying 'We are shortly getting another Scots Guards Company', the attachment never in fact materialised. Coldstream reinforcements from home and Scots Guards casualties on the hills before Florence had combined at the last moment, and rendered unnecessary the kind of composite Battalion which had so distinguished itself as to win a Battle Honour for both Regiments at Barrosa one hundred and thirty years before.

For 10 days after the fall of Arezzo the Battalion remained in the area at rest and on the morning of the last day, 26 July, 'S' Company provided a party to line the route on the occasion of King George VI's visit to that part of the front. That evening, under Major R.L. Coke, who had come forward to replace Captain Neilson, they moved with the remainder of the Battalion to Montevarchi, eighteen miles down the valley of the Arno. Here they stayed for the rest of the month, watching the right flank of the Division lest the enemy should descend from out of the 5,000 ft. peaks of the Prato Magno and cause trouble in what was almost a 'back area'. No such threat, however, developed and on 1 August, First Guards Brigade, now under the command of Brigadier C.A. Montagu-Douglas-Scott, took over the van of the Divisional advance and on the following morning the Coldstream found themselves once more in the lead. Their route lay along the foothills of the Prato Magno on the Eastern side of the beautiful Arno valley; a mass of luxuriant vineyards, cool orchards and golden cornfields bathed by the August sun and waiting for the harvest. It was all too easy to forget the war amongst such glorious surroundings, but by midday on the 4 August, 'S' Company were under shell

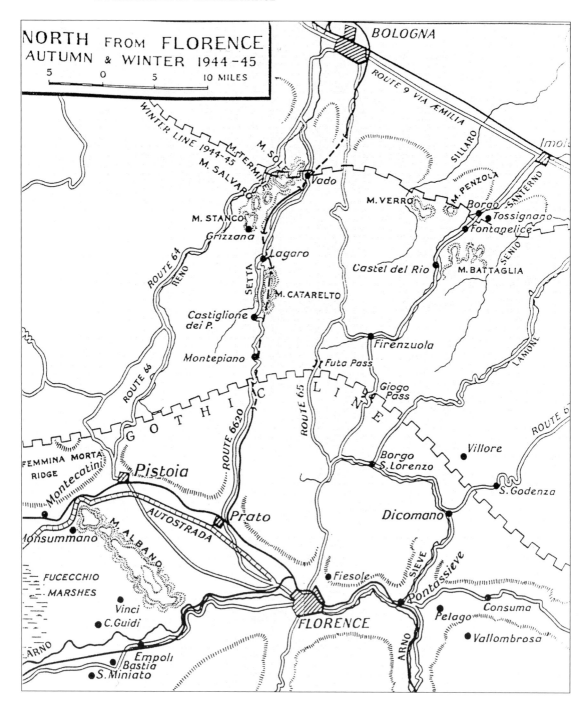

NORTH FROM FLORENCE
AUTUMN & WINTER 1944-45

5   0   5   10 MILES

BOLOGNA

ROUTE 9 VIA ÆMILIA

WINTER LINE 1944-45

M.TERMINE

M. SOLE

M. SALVARO

Vado

SILLARO

Imola

SANTERNO

M. PENZOLA

M.VERRO

Borgo

Tossignano

Fontanelice

M. STANCO

Grizzana

ROUTE 64

RENO

Lagaro

SETTA

M. CATARELTO

Castel del Rio

M. BATTAGLIA

SENIO

Castiglione
dei P.

ROUTE 66

Montepiano

Firenzuola

LAMONE

Futa Pass

Giogo
Pass

ROUTE 6620

ROUTE 65

G O T H I C   L I N E

ROUTE 6

Villore

FEMMINA MORTA
RIDGE

Montecatini

Pistoia

Borgo
S.Lorenzo

S.Godenza

AUTOSTRADA

Prato

Dicomano

Monsummano

M. ALBANO

SIEVE

Fiesole

Pontassieve

Consuma

Vinci

C.Guidi

FUCECCHIO
MARSHES

FLORENCE

Pelago

Vallombrosa

ARNO

Empoli
Bastia
S.Miniato

ARNO

fire again in the village of Cancelli after two days of cautious advances and extensive and tiring patrolling. Only 12 miles away across the Chianti hills to the West, the First Battalion Scots Guards were pushing their first cautious patrols into the suburbs of Florence.

Increased enemy shelling and mined verges to all roads and tracks made the next few days extremely unpleasant. 'S' Company lost their Company Quartermaster Sergeant, McLay, when his carrier, in which he was bringing up the rations, blew up on a road which had been swept of mines only the night before. Further back the Divisional Commander, Major General G.W.R. Templer, was severely wounded when a Grenadier truck which he was following in his car ran over another mine which blew its load, which included a piano, right on top of him. Brigadier Scott at once took his place at Divisional Headquarters and Lieutenant Colonel E.J.B. Nelson of Third Grenadiers assumed command of the Brigade. Meanwhile every effort was being made to press on and 'S' Company, in an attempt to by-pass the enemy held village of Santa Agata, came under heavy shell and mortar fire in the open. Lieutenant Lloyd Johnes, who had only rejoined the Company nine days before, was here severely wounded in the leg by a mortar bomb just as he was in the act of firing a PIAT at the enemy. For two more days the lovely valley was rent with the continual concussion of bursting shells and criss-crossed at night by streams of tracer as each side poured fire upon the other. An attack by a Coldstream Company on the next village of La Torre was not successful. This village was surrounded by bare slopes and in spite of being ordered to dig in short of Torre, Major Skimming found himself very close to British artillery shelling, some of which fell short and one shell killed Lieutenant Rudd. It was clear that it was a difficult position to resupply, so the company withdrew to Villa Bonsi and on the night of 9 August the 7th Battalion Rifle Brigade came up to relieve them.

The next three days were spent at San Mazzano, a gigantic and extremely vulgar villa, beside the River Arno, where the whole battalion rested and two badly needed Platoon Commanders joined, Lieutenant I.J. Fraser from the 1st Battalion and Lieutenant J.H. Inskip from the IRTD, thus bringing the Company up to full officer strength for the first time for many weeks. Another period in the line to the North of Rignano, only 10 miles from Florence, followed, but was quite uneventful and during it Major Coke wrote home to RHQ that 'the last fortnight or so has been pretty hectic and most tiring, advancing over ghastly country, fortunately without much opposition from the Krauts. We are now halted again and sitting in quite a comfortable position, the work at present consisting mainly of doing long-range patrols and the Company is now fully rested.'

On 18 August, the Battalion was relieved by the Grenadiers and drove back to a rest area at Renacci, 15 miles back up the Arno valley, where they remained until the end of the month. Leave parties were quickly sent off to Rome and although 'S' Company were unfortunate in being recalled, almost as soon as they got there, it provided a welcome break. Those who stayed behind were able to walk out in San Giovanni, and like the First Battalion, who had spent a fortnight out of the line in Sienna earlier in the month, they found it very pleasant.

The Gothic Line
Whilst the 2nd Battalion Coldstream Guards were resting at Renacci, great changes were taking place on the Allied front. The enemy, who in the last three months had been hounded out of Rome and Florence and chased without respite across the intervening one hundred and fifty miles of jagged country, had now retired to the fortresses of their much publicised Gothic Line. General Alexander, in an attempt to break through these mountain defences before the summer finally gave way to autumn, had accordingly transferred the bulk of the Eighth Army to the Eastern sector near the Adriatic coast and on 25 August attacked. Although partly successful, his lack of superiority in manpower had failed to produce the great break-through that had been hoped for and the Allies found themselves involved in a mountain struggle at the beginning of autumn when almost on the brink of the Lombardy Plain.

As a direct result of this shift of forces to the east, much of the remainder of the Allied line was somewhat thinly held and when First Guards Brigade returned to the front on 1 September, it had to cover an extremely extended area to the east of Florence and at the same time follow up the enemy during his withdrawal into the hills. Forty miles to the west, on the other side of Florence, the First Battalion Scots Guards in 24th Guards Brigade were doing exactly the same thing. The Second Battalion Coldstream Guards moved from Renacci early on the 1 September and passed up through Rignano and Pontassieve and along Route 70 to Consuma, where, at a height of over 3,000 feet, they took over positions on the watershed of the Prato Magno from the companies of the 7th Rifle Brigade. The drive, apart from being most picturesque, was uneventful, despite the fact that the latter half was in full view of the enemy (on the hills to the north) whose reactions were so slow that their shells only hit the road after the last vehicle of a very long convoy had gone safely past.

From 'S' Company's positions on the heights above Consuma it was possible to watch the sun sink into the sea beyond Pisa, whilst in every other direction the peaks of the Apennines and the chestnut woods on the lower slopes, now in the full glory of the autumn bronze, provided a landscape as beautiful as any that they had seen before in Italy. It was not surprising that this lovely spot was rich in villas and hotels and, so long as they remained there, only the forward sections were required to live in slit trenches, the remainder sleeping warmly under blankets, for it was now pretty cold at night, and at worst on a clean and dry floor under a good substantial roof. Civilians brought in valuable information about the German positions in the Gothic Line opposite and each night patrols went out to check and seek for more. Eventually, after nine days of this very comfortable campaigning, the enemy had fallen back so far that the Brigade was withdrawn from the area of Consuma and only the Welsh Guards were left to guard that flank. The Coldstream moved down the hill, first to the area of Polago within three miles of Pontassieve, but next day, following the Grenadiers' advance up the Sieve valley, they moved again to garrison the newly captured town of Dicomano, 10 miles to the north. From here the Divisional axis swung right up Route 67 towards San Godenzo and eventually to Forli; and whilst the Grenadiers continued to advance along the hills to the South of this road, the Coldstream were directed to occupy those on the north.

Accordingly, early on the afternoon of 12 September, No. 4 Company, leapfrogging through 'S' Company, made the first contact of Sixth Armoured Division with the Gothic Line and were able to observe the enemy strolling about in their positions and putting their blankets out to dry in the sun. For weeks past the Intelligence reports had build up a frightening picture of the strength of this famous defensive work, but now that it was at last in sight, it was quite plain for all to see that the formidable barbed wire was in fact rotten and rusty, the camouflage was peeling off the pill boxes and many of the positions hopelessly waterlogged. Patrols which went up to the wire that evening could see or hear little of the enemy and within the next few days it became clear that once again the Germans had withdrawn. However, this time a common enough event assumed far more significant proportions. 'They can usually be relied upon to beat it 12 hours before our arrival', wrote Lieutenant Fraser, but now the Gothic Line itself had been abandoned and Kesselring, weakened by the Eighth Army's attack in the east, had been forced to pull back from his much-vaunted positions and withdraw to a shorter and more economical line of defence in the peaks of the mountains further to the north.

Meanwhile, Second United States Corps had opened its attack over the Futa

Pass to the West and, in conformity with this advance, First Guards Brigade were ordered to 'lean upon the enemy'. As far as 'S' Company and the 2nd Battalion Coldstream Guards were concerned, this meant an advance across country, starting on the 15th, through the Gothic Line positions to occupy the village of Villore and the high ground beyond. There was no opposition to this move except from thickly sown mines which very nearly caused 'S' Company the loss of two more of its officers, when Lieutenant Fraser, walking with Major Coke, trod on one of the smaller anti-personnel variety. 'We knew we had four and a half seconds in which to do something before the little horror jumped into the air to scatter its load of ball bearings at all and sundry', wrote Lieutenant Fraser of the affair. They both dived for cover, one behind a rather slender tree, and the other beside an entirely inadequate bank; but before they were on the ground, the mine jumped. 'I saw its shadow', Lieutenant Fraser goes on, 'and then it just fell down again. It was a most awful anti-climax and I imagine that we owe the intactness of various parts of our anatomy to some nameless Czech who kindly omitted to put in the detonator.'

The Battalion pressed on into the hills, until on 17 September, they were relieved by a battalion of the Eighth Punjab Regiment in a place where 'S' Company were 'three hours march from the nearest point that a jeep could get to and about 2,500 feet up. All supplies had to come by mule and one dark night several of them fell over a cliff.' This latter comment, taken from a letter home, was typical of the lack of pity shown to these miserable but essential animals on which so much depended in the mountains. From another such letter comes the opinion that jeeps were far more reliable, 'as the mules are managed by flighty Italians whose next move can never be predicted'. Despite their unpopularity, both the mules and their handlers were to become very much a part of 'S' Company's life during the next few months in the mountains and on several occasions they could not easily have managed without them.

In the east, the Eighth Army, still attempting to keep up the impetus of its attack towards Rimini and the rolling plains beyond, was needing more men and the 10th Indian Division, who were holding a mountain front to the east of the upper Arno valley, were ordered to its assistance. First Guards Brigade, who had now leaned against the enemy for long enough, were accordingly transferred to X Corps to fill this gap; and, on 19 September the 2nd Battalion Coldstream Guards took over positions on Monte Penna, a 4,000 foot mountain covered with beech woods and crowned by a great monastery, eighteen miles to the north of Arezzo. Deep and vigorous patrols were at once sent out to discover where the enemy might be. No contact was made and on the 22 September, after the withdrawal of all German forces from the X Corps front had been firmly established, the Battalion handed over its positions to some anti-aircraft gunners and moved back to a concentration area only four miles from the pleasant town of Arezzo.

Letter from Italy
Major R.L. Coke   *'S' Coy. attchd. Coldstream Guards*

I arrived here three or four days ago from IRTD, which I was thankful to leave at long last and thought you might like to hear what news I can give you of this company.

One's general impression is that it is a very good company in excellent heart and with some very good NCOs and Guardsmen, all very keen. There is no doubt that most of the credit for this happy state of affairs should go to Andrew Neilson, who was very popular and is much missed by everyone. It was very sad about his death and also that of CSM Brown, who one gathers did very well indeed too.

The new CSM is Young, who was a Platoon Sergeant and seems an excellent man. Sgt. Copeland appears to be an outstanding Platoon Sergeant and the others too seem to be good.

The Officers as you know are:- Colin Dalrymple 2 i/c, Jack Lloyd-Johnes and Jim Wilson, all of whom I am quite happy about.

Neil Douglas and Robin Nunneley whom we heard were at the CRU have both gone on to 1st Battalion Scots Guards and so I expect we shall get Gerald Winter from IRTD, as I think he is the only fit subaltern there at the moment.

We are up to strength in other ranks having today got 10 men from CRU.

I also want to get at least one set of pipes and preferably two out of 1st Battalion Scots Guards. I have got 1 Piper (Watson) who luckily has his own set of pipes with him; there are also 2 other men in the company who are good Pipers, but we've no pipes for them. I feel that the Regiment might provide us with at least one set of pipes. If you agree to this perhaps it would help if you wrote to Col. Derek and brought a little pressure to bear!

I thought an appropriate company march might be that new tune 'The Roads that lead to Rome', but I've not heard it played and Watson doesn't know it, so in the meantime until we've discovered whether it is good or bad, we're going to have '79th's Farewell to Gibraltar'.

The Coldstream like the pipes very much and I think it would be a splendid thing if we could have at least two sets in the company.

Do write if you can find time and give us all the news, especially of 3rd Battalion Scots Guards.

Have just heard that Col. Billy is out here and will be coming to see us so will talk to him about the pipes!

A letter from RHQ Scots Guards London to the Author's Mother

25 Buckingham Gate
5 September 1944

Dear Mrs Curtis,
A week ago I heard some news which I hoped would prove to be correct and today I learn that it is. Richard Coke, who succeeded Andrew, tells me in a letter dated 28 August that Andrew has received the immediate award of the DSO.

If he is allowed to say so it must have been gazetted and the War Office confirmed this, but it has not yet been published, but you may take it that it is all right. When the Lieutenant Colonel was in Italy in early August he knew that he had been recommended for it.

This may be a small consolation to you and your sister. It is, at the least, the hallmark of his work and achievement for the Regiment.

I think I am right in saying that only one other Company Commander in the Regiment has won the DSO during this war – Jock Macrae – and he too was killed. A DSO in the Brigade of Guards only goes to those rare spirits like him and Andrew – their name is not legion it is immortal.

Yours very sincerely, Archie Pearson.

LIEUT I.J. FRASER   'S' COY. SCOTS GUARDS   17 Sept. 44

We have just finished a rather sudorific week of advance through the most difficult country imaginable. We have been leap-frogging from hill to hill through a kind of upland plateau intersected with gullies and ravines, such that our altitude is continually oscillating between 500 and 2500 ft. My Platoon captured two of these hills, the second it was asserted, being a bastion of the Gothic Line. However, it was taken by a reconnaissance party of 3 men, an action which, though brilliantly planned and executed under the direction of a master of the military art, was greatly aided by the total absence of the defenders.

The Germans are very obliging in this manner they can be relied upon to beat it at least 12 hours before our arrival. Consequently in a week's 'bitterly contested advance by some of the best trained troops in the British Army through country presenting almost insurmountable obstacles to the problem of supply' (B.B.C.) our only casualties have been due to blisters and the kicks of our mules.

MAJ. R.L. COKE, MC 'S' COY. SCOTS GUARDS, C.M.F.   24 Sept. 44

We are out of the line for a few days, having had a very strenuous fortnight or so in various parts and in and out of the Gothic Line. It is really wicked country in the heat of the day in full equipment etc. and of course it is pretty cold at night. We did a lot of pushing forward, but luckily never had to fight much. The

Germans had always just withdrawn in time, which was just as well, as a few spandaus in that sort of country are quite enough to cause a lot of trouble.

My last company position was three hours march from the nearest place a jeep could get to and about two and a half thousand feet up. All supplies etc. by mule, and one dark night several of them fell over a cliff as the path was very narrow and bad.

I hope we soon see the last of the Apennines and all other mountains for that matter. I think the sooner we get into the Lombardy Plain the better, and we all hope the war will be over before we reach the Alps.

CSM Young has got a DCM and Sgt. McPhail a MM. These came through about three days ago and I think are for the Ornito battle. Both are excellent men in every way and well deserve them.

I went over to the CRU yesterday and brought back with me a L/Sgt. Allardyce. I am told he is a good man. Dick Hunter is also there and a subaltern called Blandy, whom I had not met before.

John Inskip is a great success and is doing very well here.

Jim Wilson got some kind of fever and went to hospital a couple of days ago, but I think will be back with us in 3 or 4 days.

CHAPTER 7

Monte Battaglia, September/October 1944

After five days of rest, the Brigade reverted once again to Sixth Armoured Division and on the 27 September the Battalion moved back to Pelago to take over exactly the same positions as they had occupied only three weeks before. Sickness, in the form of jaundice, was meanwhile playing havoc with the officers and throughout the next month Captain Dalrymple and all the Platoon Commanders were away in hospital for varying periods. Lieutenant P.J.B. Blandy, who came up as a reinforcement just before the Company moved, was therefore doubly welcome. The next three days were spent waiting about at Pelago for the expected orders to move with Sixth Armoured Division over the Futa Pass towards Bologna, with the added hope that they would get to

The Track leading up to Monte Battaglia 2003

The Memorial Plaque on Monte Battaglia 2003

that city before 24th Guards Brigade, who were already half way there along the road from Prato. However, they were to be disappointed; for the weather in the mountains and urgent calls for assistance elsewhere had caused this advance to be postponed and once again 1st Guards Brigade were detached from the Division for an independent role. This time they received orders to take over positions from a battalion of the 88th United States Division on Monte Battaglia, a 2,000 foot peak on the Northern fringe of the Apennines only twelve miles from Imola, a town on the edge of the Lombardy Plain.

They moved on the morning of 2 October in pouring rain which cascaded down upon the Battalion from a cold and lowering sky, as they wound their way up into the mountains along a road which runs to the East of the Futa Pass, through Firenzuola and eventually down to Imola and the plain.

The convoy stopped two miles short of the village of Castel del Rio by the side of the swollen Santerno River and there, huddled under groundsheets in the lee of their vehicles, the Battalion ate the most welcome hot meal they were to get for almost three weeks. Thus refreshed, the companies set off, soon after darkness had fallen, on the long walk up the slippery rain-swept mountain track which led to their concentration area, where, under a continual downpour, they slept the night in some sodden upland fields. To add to these miserable conditions, the enemy shelled the area during the night and, although most of their rounds fell clear of where the Battalion was, one landed on 'S' Company and killed Guardsman Lingwood, the stretcher bearer who had won a Military Medal for his gallantry on Monte Piccolo in the previous May. Next morning, there was some delay whilst the Germans put in an unsuccessful attack against the Americans, but shortly after midday two Coldstream companies went forward to take over the advanced positions on Monte Battaglia, leaving 'S' Company behind to help with the mules. By 6 October, they too had gone forward, 1st Guards Brigade's 'take over' was complete and the unpleasantness of the situation had become apparent to all.

'Battaglia was a ridge some 2,400 feet high, running from South to North and culminating at its Northern point in a ruined castle. From this castle, two ridges, Cornezzano and Poseggio, radiated to east and west, both bending round to the south, so that the whole feature resembled an anchor with its head towards the enemy. The castle and central ridge were held by the Brigade; Cornezzano and Poseggio were still in German hands and had been used as bases for desperate counter-attacks to regain the Battaglia ridge' ('The Coldstream Guards 1920-1946'). At the outset, two Coldstream companies took over positions on the south-eastern slopes of Battaglia, whilst the Welsh Guards held the main ridge and the Grenadiers protected the Gunner observation post in the castle. All these positions were overlooked by the enemy from three sides and were pounded night and day by their guns and mortars, so that sleep, except from sheer exhaustion, or existence at all outside a slit trench, was barely possible. To this kind of treatment, 'S' Company were to a certain extent used, but what they had never before experienced was the rigour of the weather which accompanied it.

Their original orders had been to hold the Battaglia position for forty-eight hours, but this position subsequently stretched to no less than twenty four days, during every one of which a torrent of rain fell upon the mountain. Slit trenches filled to a depth of several feet with icy water, clothing and blankets became so wringing wet that there was no hope of drying them and the paths up which all supplies had to come were soon feet deep in slimy, treacherous mud. 'The platoon areas were filthy with old ration tins and excrement, and all around there spread a waste of mud and rock and shell-scarred tree stumps, scattered with shell-holes and the unburied corpses of German and American dead. Cooking was possible only on Tommy-cookers, and of these there were very few' ('The Coldstream Guards 1920-1946').

Throughout the three weeks of this misery, the problem of supply was one of the greatest. Mule head was at a farm house four miles from the summit of Battaglia and the small and almost impassable tracks which led between the two were accurately registered by the German guns. Matters were made no easier by the attitude of the muleteers, who, only too often, would think nothing of dumping their precious loads and riding the animals themselves even despite the fact that it was quite common for a laden mule to slip in deep mud and fall for several hundred feet over one of the many precipices. As with the passage of supplies up the mountain, so with the evacuation of the wounded to the rear, the problems were legion. The stretcher bearers, mostly Italians, would often take as long as seven hours to reach the ambulances on the main road and then only if they had escaped being hit by the incessant shell-fire and managed to avoid being bowled over with their stretchers by the howling rainstorms on the way.

For the first nine days of this formidable existence, 'S' Company remained in a position which guarded the Brigade's right flank and, with jaundice still rampant amongst the officers, they were for some days commanded by Lieutenant Fraser, with Lieutenant Blandy as his only other officer. Patrols went out to probe the enemy positions almost every night and on the 7 October, Lance-Serjeant Wilson, Guardsman Mellor and an Italian partisan, who was attached to the Company, were ambushed whilst investigating a house on the slopes of Cornezzano and were captured. Three days later, the

Germans put in an attack with a whole battalion on 'S' Company's left flank in the open daylight, as a result of which they lost eighty odd prisoners and a good many killed; one German company was accounted for completely.

On 14 October, the Second Coldstream exchanged their battered positions for the responsibility for the area of the Castle and prepared for an attack on Cornezzano. Meanwhile, the Americans, whom they had relieved on Battaglia, were now attacking up Route 65 towards Bologna and as a result enemy troops were drawn away from the Brigade front and life became slightly quieter. The new positions, however, were more difficult to supply than ever and rations had to be sent up in haversacks and handed up the steepest places. Nevertheless, there were some compensations, for the weather now began to improve and despite the odd hundred mortar bombs which fell on 'S' Company area every day, living conditions became more bearable. On the 15 October, the Company took over positions on Battaglia West and sent out almost nightly patrols to probe the enemy defences on the Cornezzano ridge opposite. These were usually only very small parties and one such, consisting of Lieutenant Blandy and one Guardsman, spent most of a night listening to a conversation between two German sentries on the top of the ridge. From information gained by these patrols an attack by a series of larger parties was organised for the night of the 20/21 October, but when the darkness came down, accompanied by blinding rain it was decided that the tricky ascent would not be possible under such conditions and the attack was postponed.

Next day, two Divisional Commanders, Generals Murray of Sixth Armoured and Laver of the First Division, accompanied by the Brigade Commander, Commanding Officer and all the Company Commanders, appeared in 'S' Company area to view the ground ahead and to coordinate plans for a joint attack. Such a gathering of distinguished visitors is never very popular with front line troops and, sure enough, within a few minutes of their dispersal, 'S' Company was briskly shelled for 10 minutes and the now absent visitors roundly cursed for as many more. However, though 'S' Company were reluctant to see it, some good had come out of the gathering, for the Generals had decided that, weather permitting, Monte Cornezzano should be taken on the following night. Unfortunately, 22 October was a day of mist and rain and when evening came the weather certainly did not permit an attack, although a patrol was sent out to confirm apparent signs that the enemy were withdrawing along the whole front.

Apart from a great many mines, this patrol found the German positions empty and on the evening of the 23 October a company of the King's Shropshire Light Infantry took over Cornezzano and on the following day the

Second Coldstream were relieved. Transport was waiting at Castel del Rio to take them to billets in the little mountain village of Casa Melina which was several miles back along the main road and here, they found their accommodation 'far from luxurious, but after Battaglia a pigsty would have been welcome'.

After nine days out of the line, the Battalion went forward to a changed front; but although their axis of advance had now altered to the Senio valley, the next to the east from the Santerno, their surroundings were depressingly familiar. 'S' Company took over positions amongst the old German ones on Monte Cornezzano; arriving there just before midnight after a gruelling march from Castel del Rio in pitch darkness and pouring rain. Their supporting mules were quite defeated by the gradient and the mud and had to be left behind at Battalion Tactical Headquarters until morning. The nearest Coldstream company was half a mile away under the forbidding cliffs of Battaglia and 'S' Company had every right to feel a trifle lonely. However, there was no shelling at all on the following day, a remarkable event after the continual battering of the previous month. The Company maintained a standing patrol out in front of their main position during this period, but it had little to report except on one night when the enemy suddenly shelled and machine-gunned it with enthusiasm and wounded one Guardsman in the leg. That very same night a cold wind blew across the mountains and with it came the first snow of the winter – two inches, which soon disappeared.

After eight days of very cold inactivity the Battalion were relieved by the Welsh Guards on the night of 11 November and, greatly assisted by some 'artificial moonlight', 'S' Company tramped back the eight weary miles to Palazzuolo, arriving there at four in the morning, cold, hungry and utterly exhausted. Mobile baths and a change of clothes appeared later in the day and soon afterwards came the most welcome sight of all, the battalion transport arrived. Few remembered the bumpy journey back over the watershed to Borgo San Lorenzo and by nightfall, when all were settled into billets in the Sieve valley about twenty miles from Florence, no battalion had ever slept sounder.

Whilst 'S' Company had been fighting in the mountains, the question of their continued attachment to the Second Coldstream had been very much a matter of discussion amongst the 'powers that be' at home. The General Commanding the Brigade of Guards had actually told Major Coke during his visit to the Italian front in October that 'S' Company would shortly have to leave the battalion and be made available as reinforcements for the First Battalion Scots Guards. This news, which was not publicised, was a hard blow to 'S' Company, for the links which bound them to their foster battalion after eight months of hard service together were very strong, and it was a proud man who walked out in Florence or in Rome wearing on his arm the multicoloured insignia of a blue and gold Scots Guards shoulder title, the red numerals of the Second Coldstream and the black and white 'mailed fist' of the Sixth Armoured Division.

Much to everyone's relief, the plan to remove 'S' Company from the Second Coldstream during October never finally materialised and amongst the delights of Florence and the joy of being out of the mountains for a short space the whole idea was forgotten. Meanwhile Lieutenants Wilson and Inskip had returned to the Company from hospital and, with Lieutenant Fraser still going strong as the third Platoon Commander, Lieutenant Blandy became without a platoon and was quickly snatched up by the First Battalion who, amongst the bleak hills of the Setta valley, were rapidly running all too short of experienced junior leaders.

LETTER FROM MAJ. R.L. COKE, MC   'S' COY. S.G. ATT. C.G.
15 Oct. 44

I got your letter dated 7 Oct. today. We were very glad to hear the news. I am sorry poor Feathers has had such a rough time with his Company.

A lot has happened here since I last wrote to you and I will try and tell you all about it in chronological order! Jim Wilson developed jaundice in hospital about 25 Sept. and I immediately got the only remaining subaltern Officer from CRU – Peter Blandy – to replace him.

I had a bad cold myself and lost my voice completely for three days – had a Company Drill Parade one day and had to get John Inskip to stand beside me and do the shouting as I just couldn't utter a thing! On the strength of this and of course also the fact that I was due for it (!) I managed to get a week's leave to recover and off I went to Rome, the battalion being out of the line, and we were told if they were committed at all it would only be a 'holding' role.

I had a little more than one clear day in Rome before being recalled, because it turned out Colin Dalrymple had gone and got this beastly jaundice – blast him.

Rome was very gay and tremendous fun. I can't remember if I told you about it before, but as a result of a party we had when I took the whole company to Rome about six weeks ago, two or three girls had said they would make us a Company Flag. I never thought much would come of this as it was decided about 3 a.m. one morning and anyway they had nothing to copy from.

Much to my surprise this time I found the thing all finished and ready with a very smart card to go with it suitably inscribed and signed etc.

The flag is really a very beautiful affair – all silk with a rather too large Scots Guards star in the middle. The silk is in the brigade colours (and the right colours!) the star is almost perfect, the only thing is that the thistle is rather a miserable affair – I suppose a Roman thistle and not a Scotch one! It is much too good a thing to use as a company flag and anyway wouldn't stand the weather and no doubt too it is entirely the wrong thing for a mere Company to have, so at present we are using it as a decoration in the Coy. Officers' Mess. I imagine it is probably the only Regimental Colour ever to have been made in Rome and I think really quite a good effort on the part of the Italians!

On my way back I saw Col. Derek (Cardiff) and also Tom Harvey (slightly wounded but in excellent form) in Florence and heard all about their battle, which sounded a magnificent performance.

I found the Battalion and 'S' Company flung in to hold a pretty awful place about eight miles march from a road along a ghastly track often 8-10' deep in mud. The weather was bad and it rained incessantly – everyone permanently soaked to the skin. John Inskip had also got this damned jaundice and gone to hospital, which left Ian Fraser Commanding and Peter Blandy as the only other Officer.

Two of our chaps, L/Sgt Wilson and Mellor, together with a little Italian partisan (Bruno) we had picked up earlier were missing off a Recce Patrol. They were the only 3 on the patrol and from information I got later from some Italian civilians I think there is little doubt that they ran right into a German ambush. I think there is a good chance both our people may be prisoners – I don't care to think of what may have happened to the wretched Italian, who was not a bad boy as Italians go. I am afraid the best that one can hope for him is that he met a quick death!

Except for the weather and the awful supply problem, things might have been worse. We took a sergeant prisoner who came one night on a Recce Patrol to find out about us. He was a fine soldier no doubt, with 2 iron crosses etc. but a very keen Nazi and an absolute swine of a man.

The same night as we caught the sergeant, the Germans put in quite a big attack on the positions on our left, held by the Welsh Guards. The Germans made an awful mess of it all and got caught in the open in the daylight and a good many were killed or captured. Welsh Guards casualties were, I believe, 1 killed and 2 wounded – quite a successful little affair! I wish the Germans would put in more counter-attacks like that as it is much the easiest way of killing them.

My Company is just off up the hill again this afternoon for another spell. I dread the awful five hours' march! Hope the weather holds fine, it is such hell when it rains and the slit trenches are all full of water!

EXCERPTS FROM DIARIES OF MAJOR R.L. COKE, MC

7 Oct.1944
The news looks as if the Bde might have to stay up in these wilds for some days yet. The Maj. General (Budget Lloyd) is over here and will have to settle about what is to happen to the Brigade of Guards in Italy and 'S' Company in

particular – quite a knotty problem for him!

Germany was raided today between the hours of 12-1 p.m. by 3000 heavy bombers escorted by 2000 fighters.

No. 2 Company have been having a bad time with a good deal of shelling. 'S' Company went into the line last night and things are fairly quiet so far. They had been used for bringing up mules etc. before. More rain during the night. The track is a quagmire, no longer passable to jeeps.

The Americans, whom we relieved, were lucky and had fine weather, but there were apparently far too many of them on the ground and swanning about, and they had very heavy casualties.

8 October 1944 (Sunday)
Set off for Tac HQ about another four miles on down the track with Sgt. Ions, leaving Rigby behind to wait for the mules coming up this evening to bring our packs and greatcoats. Miserable march, it rained all the way and we slithered along in the mud.

Arrived Tac HQ about 12 a.m. Saw Billy Steele, who is commanding as Col. Bob still on leave in Cairo – I personally wish Billy would get command, as think he is better and certainly nicer.

Found the Company on the ridge running due south of M. Battaglia.

Fairly quiet so far, though the castle on M. Battaglia gets shelled a lot. Pouring with rain and every one soaked through, otherwise in good spirits. I am in command with Peter Blandy as the only other officer, and he is feeling ill and looks like going sick.

7 and 8 platoons + Coy HQ in position, the other platoon (9) being still used for portering. I did not see them on the way up.

Very little known of the German positions as apparently the Americans did no patrolling. Poured with rain all day and all night. We spent a very miserable night in the open. I managed to get an hour or two's sleep, sitting down in my gas cape and steel hat. Slit trenches all full of water etc.

9 October 1944 (Monday)
Rained all night and for several hours this morning. All very miserable, soaked through and covered with mud. Cleared up about 10.30 am. Sun came out for rest of the day and dried us up nicely. 2 Company who have had a rough time, what with shelling, and the weather, were relieved last night by some Welsh Guards.

Billy Steele was ordered by Brigade to find out more about what is going on on Cornazzano (Pt 620). May have to send Ian Fraser out tonight. Very awkward place to get at with almost precipitous sides. Don't want to have a repetition of L/Sgt Wilson's patrol. We did a recce and Billy very sensible and fully realised the dangers and difficulties.

Luckily when we returned we found a Pole who had deserted and been brought in, who gave us full information about the position on Cornazzano, which is strongly held by a Bn of Germans. He gave us their exact positions, also where their Coy and Bn HQ are and everything we wanted to know. This ruled out the necessity of sending out Ian, who obviously couldn't get anything like as much information from a patrol.

Bob Chinner and I laid on a good stonking programme and let them have it good and proper.

4 Company are relieved tonight by Welsh Guards, and Coldstream Guards Tac goes back too. We are to be under command of Welsh Guards (Col Jocelyn G) and stay up here for a few days more.

Bruce Kennedy (Capt. Ayrshire Yeomanry) relieved Bob Chinner, AyrshireYeomanry (Lieutenant, Forward Observation Officer). Bruce turned out to be Deb Birkbeck's husband, funny place to meet on top of the Apennines! He seems a nice and capable chap, though doesn't look too strong. His father owns a big saw milling firm. He is interested in trees, but doesn't know much about the growing of them, I fancy. We had a long talk about Westacre and trees, etc.

10 October 1944 (Tuesday)
Quiet night and fine until about 3 a.m. in morning when it started to rain, but I got in a good sleep before the rain came and made life miserable again! About 3.30 a.m. we heard some small arms firing which turned out later to be a German raid on the house where the Grenadier Guards Tac HQ are and which was formerly Coldstream Guards Tac HQ. Very bad house to choose as it is really part of the front line and under observation etc. Pretty successful from German point of view. Sentries idle or something went wrong, and the Germans got right up and threw grenades through the windows.

Douglas Berry died of wounds and another officer wounded, and eight or 10 other casualties. Poor Hill got rather a shaking up. He was my Company runner at Grenadier Guards Tac. HQ.

Rain stopped but dull and cold until afternoon when the sun came out. Some shelling during the afternoon and a direct hit on R.A.P. House. The Company had no casualties.

We were told that we would be relieved tomorrow night by 2 platoons of Grenadier Guards who have been about six days in the Castle and so will not be in any too good fettle I expect. They in turn are being relieved by a platoon of 3 Company Coldstream Guards and 9 platoon 'S' Company under the command of David Toler. Don't like this much as there is no officer with 9 platoon at present.

As it was getting dark we were warned that about 150 Germans were advancing roughly in our direction, and that we must expect to be attacked. I warned everyone, and then got some rest. The Germans shelled us intermittently with what sounded like a 105 mm. Some shells fairly close, but no casualties.

About 3.30 a.m. I was woken up by L/Sgt. Mullens, who brought along a prisoner captured by L/Corporal Imrie and Davie who had been on sentry in their trench. This German, a Feldwebel (full Sgt.) was on a recce patrol with two others, who unfortunately got away. He was easily dealt with by L/Corporal Imrie! He turned out to be a very arrogant Nazi and had won the

Iron Cross twice. He had a diary, from which I gathered he'd been at Anzio, etc. Loot from him comprised a schmeizer, a pair of field glasses not in very good condition but can easily be put right, an Iron Cross and some money. He was from 2 Coy 725 Regiment; he would give us no other information.

Shortly after he came in, a lot of firing broke out from the direction of the Castle and the RAP etc. This turned out to be quite a strong German counter attack, and the Welsh and Grenadiers took some 80 odd prisoners and no doubt killed a good few. Our losses were one killed and two wounded. That'll calm them for a bit!

Col. Jocelyn Gurney came to see me during the morning.

11 October 1944 (Wednesday)

Great excitement over the counter attack last night, which was repulsed with heavy loss etc. We got mortared a bit during morning. Say got a small piece in his back, but it doesn't seem to have done him much harm, otherwise no one hit.

David Gibson-Watt is coming up to take this position over from the Grenadiers the day after tomorrow. Had lunch with me. Had never really met him properly before. He seems a very nice fellow. Told me that John de Rutzen was killed by a shell this morning between the RAP and Welsh Tac HQ.

Tony Denny and about 38 scratch Grenadiers relieved us. They were late, should have turned up about 1 a.m., but didn't arrive until 3 a.m. Perhaps just as well as the Germans had been shelling the track a good deal, and they had quietened down by the time we had to use it.

9 platoon tonight go up to the Castle Area with a platoon from 3 Company all under command of David Toler, hope they will be all right. Am very worried as there is no Scots Guards officer with them. Remainder of Company got out and back to main HQ at Val Maggiore, just as it was getting light.

We were all dead tired on arrival there after a two and a half hour march along that track about 6" deep in sticky mud in most places. Very hard work! I was feeling rotten and felt as if I had a cold coming on. Found Humpo Fitzroy at Val Maggiore who had got some tea ready for the whole Company. This was most welcome. We rested there for about an hour and then went on down the hill to the main road arriving there about 0830 hrs. Into TCV's waiting there and back about four miles to a billet area in a house.

12 October 1944 (Thursday)

Very tired after no sleep last night. We all had a mobile bath, but clean clothes difficult! Col. Bob back from Cairo at last! Jim Eagan came to dinner, we drank quite a lot of the Kummel that Col. Bob had brought back with him. Got letters from Nial O'Neill and one dated Oct. 1st from Mummy, also from Colin in hospital in Rome! Also a letter from the Pay Office people about my claim for loss of kit put in via 2 S.G. about a year ago. They have not heard anything of it! Must write to Greenwood.

13 October 1944 (Friday)

Quiet day. No. 4 Company left their billets to go up the hill. 2 & 4 Companies are to attack & occupy the ridge to the north of M. Battaglia the night of 14 – 15 October. Billy Steele told me that the Maj.-General had definitely decided that 'S' Coy should leave 2nd Battalion Coldstream Guards and be available for 1st Battalion Scots Guards. They are to be replaced by a Company of Queens! I shall reserve judgement on this until I see what is to happen to the Company!

We moved into the house which 4 Company had had and are quite comfortable. My cold, thank heavens, has gone before it had much chance to break out properly. Have to walk about in my old suit of battle dress and a stocking cap! As my smart things all at 'A' echelon.

Lorna Twining came to lunch with us and is going to come again on Sunday and bring some buns for the Company. Bill Harris and Michael Hollings went up the hill to form a rear HQ somewhere. Got a bundle of papers from Jean (about the last I fear), also a silver cigar holder from Mummy.

John Pope, Billy Steele, Bob Southey, Ian, Peter and I were the only officers in to dinner. We made some rum punch and drank a lot of it which did us good. Wrote Mummy an AML.

14 October 1944 (Saturday)

Fine day again, quite hot! The last few days have made a big difference to the mule track. Billy Steele, John Pope and I went to Brigade HQ after lunch to find out the form. Saw the Brigadier; apparently plans are changed every hour or so. Looks as if we may have to go up soon again and take over from David Toler's people.

78 Division attack etc. has been put off 24 hrs, also 2 & 4 Companies' attack.

Ian Fraser went to 'A' echelon and came back with my beret and smart suit of battle dress. He said Jamie Leveson (Capt. The Lord Leveson, MC, Coldstream Guards, later 5th Earl Granville) had been using my PU and keeping Gardner up until all hours! Damned cheek! I wrote him a very sharp note.

Got an interesting letter from Archie (Major A.D.B. Pearson, S.G.), also letters from Mummy, Hersey, Bridget, Aunt Mabel and John Inskip. Poor Feathers' Company (X Company), now with 1st Battalion Welsh Guards, have had a bad time and lost all their platoon commanders.

The Ayrshire Yeomany padre came over and we had a service in the house at 5.30 p.m. We were warned that we would probably have to move up tomorrow. Saw Lingwood's grave on side of road between mulehead and the long Bailey bridge.

15 October 1944 (Sunday)

I left billet area after lunch with 7 & 8 platoon + Coy HQ, some 80 strong in all. We are to take over from 'Toler Force' on ridge west of castle on Battaglia. 'Toler Force' is one platoon of 3 Company.

CHAPTER 8

Monte Penzola,
Monte Dell'Acqua Salata

On 19 November, after a week's rest, the Battalion moved back into the mountains to the all too familiar Castel del Rio sector. This time, however, they took over reserve positions for three days on the opposite side of the road from the notorious Battaglia before being moved on to hold a portion of the line on the main feature, which was graced with the cumbersome name of Monte dell'Acqua Salata. They took over from the Buffs and soon discovered that the problems of supply were to be every bit as bad as they had been on the other side of the valley. The mules were no larger, the muleteers just as unreliable and the mud as deep and treacherous as before. To make matters worse, the enemy poured almost continuous machine-gun fire on fixed lines across the one and only track, an artery of supply which was in full view of their positions by day and gained the name of 'the Causeway' since it ran along the top of a knife-edge ridge. 'Mines were reported to be sown on either side of it and its first few yards were ornamented by the decaying remains of several mules and Italian muleteer'. By day there were the usual periodic bursts of shellfire, whilst at night the sentries had an anxious time peering out from their cold and lonely slit trenches, watching and listening. Some patrols were sent out under a bright moon to keep an eye on the enemy, but generally it was a period of dull and uncomfortable existence and it was with profound relief that the Battalion gave up the area to the Grenadiers on 29 November and returned to those which they had previously occupied further to the rear. During the week 'S' Company had caught four German prisoners and had suffered two men killed when a mortar bomb had scored a direct hit on a slit trench. 'We were lucky not to have had more casualties', wrote Major Coke, 'as it was a particularly nasty bit of the front with a lot of shelling and mortaring'. By the time his letter had reached England his luck had changed.

On clear days, which were infrequent, it was possible to see the great expanse of the Lombardy Plain from the highest ground in the First Guards Brigade area and, on the horizon, the peaks of the Alps were just discernible as a blue and white shadow in the dimmest distance. Imola, at the foot of the Santerno valley, was only eight miles away and to anyone who had not undergone the rigours of Apennine campaigning in the winter, it must have seemed remarkable that the Allies had not broken through the last few miles of mountains long ago. However, the Germans in these last hills held on to their positions doggedly and showed not the slightest inclination to give up one yard of ground, inhospitable though it must have been. On the Santerno sector, they had blasted themselves into the sheer precipices of a particularly inaccessible feature called the Vena di Gesso, from which they could command a view down both the Santerno and the Sento valleys and most effectively block any advance towards Imola and into the plain beyond.

Sixth Armoured Division, long frustrated to the point of despair at being used as mountain infantry whilst their sister Armoured Divisions on the other side of the continent rushed hither and thither across the map, were now

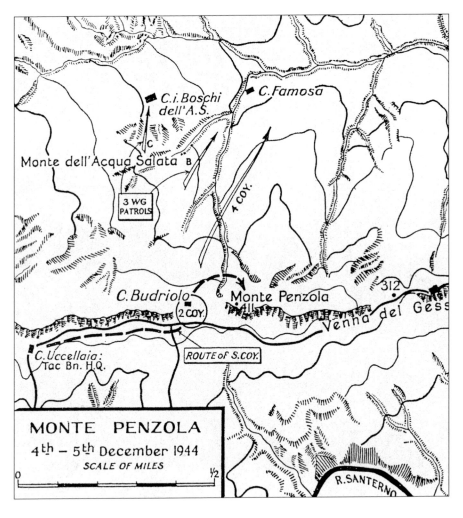

C.i.Boschi dell'A.S.

C.Famosa

Monte dell'Acqua Salata B

3 WG PATROLS

4 COY.

C.Budriolo

Monte Penzola

312

Venna del Gess

2 COY.

C.Uccellaia: Tac Bn. H.Q.

ROUTE of S.COY.

MONTE PENZOLA
4th – 5th December 1944
SCALE OF MILES
0   ½

R.SANTERNO

determined to break out into tank country before the winter finally closed in and prevented such thoughts until the spring. An advance down the Santerno valley to capture Tossignano, the last big mountain village only seven miles from the plain, was all that appeared to be necessary to start rolling an assault which might take their tanks to Venice, Trieste or even over the Alps to Vienna and who could tell where else beyond. Even the most optimistic of these planners were agreed upon one thing, however, and that was the fact that the ground over which this initial and all important attack was to go in, was completely dominated by the enemy on the Vena di Gesso and particularly by those of his positions on Monte Penzola, one of its peaks. No attack on Tossignano could even be considered until Penzola was in Allied hands and on 1 December this task was allotted to the Second Coldstream.

The south side of the Penzola Venna del Gesso range from Gesso farmhouse 2003

'Penzola rose from the cliff face of the Vena di Gesso, a little Matterhorn 1,300 feet high, and up its steep cliffs a frontal assault would have been barely possible'. Fortunately First Guards Brigade already held the ridge to the West and could look down on Penzola's northern slopes, whilst, as far as the rest of the mountain was concerned, an abundance of deserters and enemy prisoners and an ample supply of air photographs had combined to give a near perfect picture of the German defences. D Day for the attack was fixed for 4 December and it turned out to be one of low cloud and rain squalls which successfully grounded the projected air support and did nothing to improve the state of the ground over which the attack was to go in after dark. However, the whole artillery of the Division were in support and their guns began the opening barrage as soon as the light began to fail and kept up an incessant fire for the

whole of the next three hours. The plan of attack was simple; at least, so it sounded. Two Coldstream companies were to start off at 9.15 and seize the hill to the west of Penzola, at the same time obtaining a foothold on the north-eastern slopes. Once they were in position and their code word 'Arthur' received over the wireless at Battalion Headquarters, 'S' Company were to pass through them and assault the summit of the mountain from the rear.

The Coldstream attack went in on time and for an hour 'S' Company waited under the towering cliffs listening to the chatter of the Spandaus and the crack and whine of grenades as they pressed their way slowly up the hill. At 10.15, No. 2 Company reported themselves to be firmly in position and, although there was no news from Number 4, Colonel Coates gave the word and Major Coke led off with 'S' Company up the steep slope. The moon had now risen and in its light the pinnacle of Penzola looked even more perpendicular and unscalable than it had by day. As the Company climbed, so the ground became steeper and the mud more slippery. At times men were crawling on their hands and knees and every yard some heavily laden Guardsman would slip backwards with a crash amongst the wet and jagged rocks. Six casualties were caused by enemy shell fire as they scrambled upwards in as near silence as was possible under the circumstances and, at almost midnight, when all were dripping with sweat despite the Arctic temperature, Major Coke formed up his leading sections and led them into the final assault.

The enemy were taken completely by surprise. Most of them were keeping warm in the bottom of their dug-outs and there were no proper sentries to keep a look out. However, they were not by any means slow to recover from their shock and a fierce hand-to-hand battle was soon raging amongst the cliffs and rocks of the jagged pinnacle. The fighting was particularly severe around the enemy Company Headquarters, where the German Company Commander put up a brave but desperate resistance with his pistol, wounding several of the leading platoon, including Lieutenant Inskip, whom he shot through the eye. He also hit Guardsman Rush in the right arm. Guardsman R.J.A. Tinlin, commanding a section after its Sergeant had been wounded, distinguished himself by leading it against a strong enemy post which was holding out after all other resistance had ceased. With great dash and considerable leadership he overcame the post after a fierce fight and added a further six prisoners to the Company's already sizeable bag.

Fighting died down as quickly as it had begun, and when all was over Major Coke discovered that he had accounted for a complete German Company and had as prisoners, one officer and twenty-five men, many of whom were wounded. However, there was no time for mutual congratulation, for, as soon as the enemy on the Vena di Gesso realised that Penzola had been taken, they directed every gun and mortar that they had on to the peak. Under this terrific fire 'S' Company had to set about the task of consolidating the position and preparing themselves for the inevitable counter-attack; meanwhile it was no fun for the wounded. Reconnaissance of the only apparently feasible stretcher route to the Battalion RAP quickly disclosed a Schu minefield right across the only track and so there was nothing that could be done for the injured men who lay on the frozen and windswept summit except to wrap them up in layers of captured German greatcoats and wait for the dawn. Eventually, however, just before first light, another route was found. It missed the mine field but entailed lowering the stretchers down a slippery near perpendicular slope with a drop of fifty feet or more for anyone who made a false step.

Very soon after those wounded had started on their hazardous journey and after some more severe shelling and mortaring, the enemy put in a spirited counter-attack with elements of two companies. They attacked along the ridge from their positions on the Vena di Gesso and, by using a tremendous volume of automatic fire and a great many grenades, they managed to penetrate into Major Coke's Headquarter position. After a few very anxious moments and some very tough fighting they were thrown back with heavy loss, but not before they had killed two Guardsmen and wounded several others. Company Sergeant Major Young, who had throughout the action lived up to the glorious reputation which he had gained on Monte Lignano in July, was one of those severely wounded in this fierce close quarter fighting. A rifle grenade burst almost on him, seriously wounding him about the body and blowing off his right hand. 'Poor fellow', wrote Major Coke, 'he was wonderfully brave and cheerful. His going will be a terrible loss to the Company'.

Once repulsed with such determination, the enemy did not attack Penzola again, although they pushed their positions on the ridge closer and kept up a rain of shells. When darkness fell Major Coke, ringed his position with bee-hive mines and 'stood-to' in expectation of another attack. None came, and except for sporadic mortaring they were left alone throughout the night and for the whole of the following day. In the evening No. 2 Company came up the hill to relieve them and 'S' Company slithered wearily down the slope up which they had attacked, to take up reserve positions in the Battalion area at the bottom. Their casualties during the battle had amounted to two killed and thirteen wounded, a list far smaller than anyone had dared to expect at the outset or expected to find when the action was over. In recognition of what they had accomplished, Major Coke was later awarded the DSO, the second such decoration to go to an 'S' Company Commander, whilst Military Medals went to Lance Corporal McMinn, the stretcher bearer, and to Guardsmen Tinlin and Rush. 'The Second Coldstream have just done a first class attack and captured Penzola', wrote the Brigade Commander to London, 'the Scots Guards Company did it; first class show – everyone delighted'.

Two days later the weather broke and, in pouring rain, a Welsh Guards Company came up to take over from 'S' Company, who then moved back through Castel del Rio to the new Battalion rest area to the South of Florence. 'The depth of mud on the mule tracks was terrific and we had several men hopelessly stuck who had to be pulled out', but none minded, for they were going to rest and on the following evening the remainder of the Battalion came after them. By 12 December, the whole of the Second Coldstream, or what was left of it, were comfortably ensconced in billets in and around the village of Strada, only half an hour away from the fair city of Florence.

Venna del Gesso and Santerno Valley 2003

EXTRACT FROM WAR DIARY – ATTACK BY 2 COLDSTREAM GUARDS ON PENZOLA NIGHT 4/5 DEC. 1944

The attack on Penzola was made by 2nd Battalion Coldstream Guards and 3rd Battalion Welsh Guards Force (the latter consisting of two platoons). H hr was timed for 2115 hrs; D day 4 Dec. On 3 Dec a Chinese attack was staged, and during D day a programme of air attacks were to have been made in the area. Unfortunately bad weather grounded most aircraft, and only one mission (against C Colonna) could be flown. At H-180 the artillery programme began – during the course of the night 15,000 rounds of 25 pounder were expended.

3rd Battalion Grenadier Guards neutralised the enemy in the Camaggio area by their support weapons. In order to deceive the enemy as to the exact point threatened, the help of our neighbours was enlisted. 1 Kensingtons fired harassing machine gun tasks down the valley between 36 Infantry Brigade and 3rd Battalion Grenadier Guards positions, who also attacked and occupied Biacchi 070216.

At H hr 2 and 4 Companies 2nd Battalion Coldstream Guards and 3rd Battalion Welsh Guards force crossed the start line. Their tasks were as follows: 4 Company was to establish itself at House 048244, and on the Famosa ridge at 054244, to act as a final guard. 2 Company had as its objective Budriolo 0423, while the two 3rd Battalion Welsh Guards patrols were directed on C Boschi dell'acqua Salata 048247, and C Famosa 053248. They were to distract the enemy from the main attack, and withdraw from the area at 0400hrs. The object of these operations was to secure the rear and provide a firm base for 'S' Coy to pass through 2 Coy, and attack Penzola from the north, by way of Famosa ridge, thereby taking the Germans in the rear.

The enemy reaction to our fire was some mortaring on 1 and 2 Companies of 3rd Battalion Grenadier Guards, otherwise the only fire immediately reported was a spandau firing from Boschi dell'acqua Salata. At 2215hrs 2 Company had reached their objective, and 'S' Company began to move forward. A few minutes later DF was called down on Casetta dei Boschi 052250 in order to help the 3rd Battalion Welsh Guards Force. At 2300 hrs a fire was observed at C Famosa, and there was some shelling of 3rd Battalion Grenadier Guards area. Half an hour later 'S' Coy reported that they had reached the Famosa ridge. They found little opposition and were moving forward. At 2350 hrs 'S' Company had reached Pt 411, and were engaged in mopping up the area. By 0015hrs 10 prisoners of war had been taken, and 'S' Coy had the area firmly in their hands.

Meanwhile there had been no news received from 4 Coy 2nd Battalion Coldstream Guards or the Welsh Guards force, and it was decided that the latter would not be recalled until it was known how 4 Company had fared.

By this time 2nd Battalion Coldstream Guards Tac HQ, which had been established at C Uccellaia, came under heavy mortar fire. CM programme lessened the hostile fire, but did not completely silence the enemy. By 0200 hrs 4 Company regained contact with HQ, and were withdrawn into reserve at Uccellaia. The patrol of 'S' Company to exploit Pt 312 came under heavy fire and found the going very difficut. It was therefore withdrawn. 2nd Battalion Coldstream Guards Companies were then established as follows:- 'S' Company holding the reverse slopes of Pt 411; 4 Company with the BN HQ; 2 Company in area south and west of Pt 366. The attack had been completely successful, at a cost of two other ranks killed, one officer and eleven other ranks wounded of 'S' Company, and one other rank killed, one officer and five other ranks wounded of 4 Company.

At about 0545 hrs a counter attack was made against pt 411, from the north, but our DF effectively broke this up. Later in the morning a patrol from 'S'

Company went down towards pt 312. They saw one or two Germans in a slit trench, who refused to surrender when called upon. The patrol therefore shot one man and returned.

7 and 8 Platoons 3rd Battalion Welsh Guards successfully contained the enemy in their allotted area. 7 Platoon had originally intended to by-pass Boschi dell'acqua Salata, but they encountered two Germans in a slit trench who attempted to escape. One of these Germans was shot, but the alarm was given and the platoon was then fired on by three spandaus located, one in the gable of a house, another on the slopes of the hill and the third from the knoll, which is situated in front of the house. Rifle grenades were also shot at them, and two men were wounded. In return 7 Platoon fired back at those spandaus. During the fight the platoon had become somewhat scattered, and the platoon commander decided that he had insufficient men to attempt to raid C Famosa. He therefore remained in the area and continued to harass the enemy.

Meanwhile no 8 Platoon was moving round the right flank of the house, but the Germans here had stood to, and an additional two spandaus, one near a haystack and another from the area behind the house, shot at them. 8 Platoon fired back and later attempted to approach the house from the left flank, but was unable to do so in the face of 5 spandaus. They therefore continued to engage the enemy until the pre-arranged verey light signal announcing the success of 'S' Company went up from 3rd Battalion Grenadier Guards positions. 3rd Battalion Welsh Guards Force then withdrew. They had succeeded in giving the impression that an attack was being made down the Mescola Valley, and POWs stated that the original report was to that effect.

Excerpt from letter from Brig. A.H.D. Scott DSO   6 Dec. 44

The Battalion (Coldstream Guards) have just done a first-class attack and captured Penzola. The Scots Guards company did it; first-class show – everyone delighted.

EXCERPTS FROM THE DIARIES OF MAJOR R.L. COKE MC

3 December 1944 (Sunday)
Col Bob's O Gp to Acqua Salata from where we could see a little of the ground to N of Penzola

I managed to get his plans changed a bit for the better I think.

Now only 4 Company to go to Acqua Salata in early hours of tomorrow morning. 2 & 'S' Company to go to C Ucellaia tomorrow morning.

Arthur F-Watson and I left Acqua Salata having got this concession about 2pm and came back over the Causeway to Lothians RHQ and then on to recce the track to Casa Ucellaia.

We found it quite suitable and much better than the other way.

Very tired when we got back owing to the mud etc. We had been some way, most of it rather unnecessary!

Col Bob gave out orders at Tac at 7.30pm

Only 20 reinforcements arrived from A echelon and with no picks or shovels! Can't think what CQMS and Cpl Harwood are thinking about!

4 December 1944 (Monday)
Had my O Gp after breakfast in the church.

A good mail arrived before we left. I got letters from Mummy, Hersey and Aunt Mabel.

We left the church (Madonna del Rio) at about 3pm and climbed up past Lothians Tac HQ just below the crest of the hill, where we had about an hour to wait until it got dark enough for us to go over the top. I gave each platoon in turn a short pep talk – they all seemed in good spirits.

Carrying a fairly light order with small packs and only essential kit – no shaving kit or anything of that sort.

We went over the top of the ridge, which is in view of Penzola, at about 1730hrs behind Tac HQ and with 2 Company behind us. We took it very slowly and easily and arrived up at Casa Ucellaia (Tac HQ) at about 1900hrs.

I put the Company under the cliff in fairly safe position and we sat down to wait for H hr (2115). We watched the barrage on Penzola which seemed pretty efficient. One of our 25 pounders was dropping very short and landing quite close to us and this and the noise of the guns sent Welsby completely 'bomb-happy', much to the amusement of the others.

He lost all control and had to be sent back to RAP and evacuated.

2 Company moved off to take up their position on the cliff W of C Budriolo at 2115 hrs and 4 Company moved down at the same time from Acqua Salata bound for the Famosa ridge. I went to Tac to listen to the report on the wireless.

Arthur Farnell-Watson commanding 2 Company took longer than was expected and I did not move off until about 2215 hrs having issued a double ration of rum all round. I took the Company through a gap in the cliffs W of C Budriolo between the platoon of 2 Company in the order 9 platoon (John) Coy HQ, 8 platoon (Sgt McPhail) 7 platoon (Ian Fraser). We then made straight for Famosa ridge, aiming to hit it about 2-300 yds below the summit of Penzola. There was a bright moon, it having risen before we left Tac and visibility quite good up to about 200 yds. We advanced with 9 platoon deployed wherever ground permitted and remainder of Company in single file. As 7 Platoon were about due N of Casa Budriolo, 3 105mm shells landed in the middle of their single file killing L/Cpl Imrie and wounding Hogg, Toye, Yerbury, L/Cpl Carson, McIntosh, Docherty and McCulloch (none badly). This was obviously a German DF task as shells also dropped in a line

NS of this perimeter, fortunately there weren't very many of them! All SBs under L/Cpl McMinn stayed behind to deal with these casualties and get them safely back to Tac.

Remainder of Coy pushed on across very difficult and soft ground, up and down valleys and ridges until we got on to the Famosa ridge.

Here we had a short pause as everyone was pretty tired and then 9 pln advanced on to the summit of Pimple. Time was now 2330hrs.

Up to now there had been no sign of any Germans and it looked as if the place was unoccupied. I sent a message to that effect over the wireless from my position of observation about 60 yds from Penzola. As I did so 2 grenades exploded and TSMG fire broke out on the summit and I had to quickly send another message that it was occupied!

I at once pushed 8 Platoon through to take up position W of summit and followed them with Coy HQ and 7 Platoon. We very soon had about 10 POWs but poor John Inskip badly wounded with a bullet through the head which cracked his skull and did in his left eye and L/Sgt Dyson killed and Rush wounded with a bullet in the arm from the German Company Commander's revolver, Rush did very well and shot the Officer, firing his TSMG from his left hand and mopped up others and got his section to the top.

I then sent 7 Platoon to mop up some dugouts on the forward slope which yielded some more Germans. Consolidation was difficult as digging in most places was almost impossible owing to the rock and the reverse or south slope was almost perpendicular and very dangerous and slippery.

It was now about 0030hrs 5th Dec and all POWs and wounded were collected round my dug out and we had then to wait until the sapper party with 2 Company got a path to us through the minefield between Casa Budriolo and our position.

Soon the Germans began shelling and mortaring, most going over our ridge. Deans and one other man (a Coldstream Guard porter carrying ammo) were slightly wounded in the face by mortar bombs. The shelling made it impossible for the Royal Engineers to work on the minefield and so Sgt Marshall of 2 Company was sent round to the south to contact us and arrived at the foot of our cliff bringing with him our SBs who had returned. He arrived about 0400hrs.

Once down the cliff he reported good going back to 2 Company, Tac HQ.

We had a difficult job getting the stretcher cases down the cliff but this was done with the help of the POWs and all were got safely away.

I also sent the Coldstream Guards porters and pioneer section back in order to have less men on the position as it was difficult to find room for them.

Poor John was very brave, though he must have been in great pain and had to wait lying on the stretcher for about 4 hrs.

The men were all very cheerful at having captured the position so easily and also at getting so much loot, watches etc off the Germans.

I had all available ammo shared out and put by the slit trenches in case of a counter attack which I expected at any minute. I took the greatcoats off the

Germans and piled them over John who complained of the cold.

It was by this time very chilly and none of us had greatcoats or blankets.

At about 0500 hrs the expected counter attack came in from the north heralded by several rifle grenades which produced a squeal from one of the swine, Ian killed one with a grenade (we found his body in the morning). We brought down our DF, which I don't think hit any of them, but probably frightened them a good deal as a phenomenal number of shells were fired by the Division artillery.

Some other Germans were probably wounded by Bren and TSMG fire.

It was difficult to shoot down the forward slope without exposing one's head and shoulders on the skyline and except for one or two slits so sited, the majority of the men were slightly on the reverse slope waiting in case the Germans should gain the top of the ridge when they would have received a hot reception. However, they never got as far as this.

We had to evacuate CSM Young and L/Cpl Jones and again L/Cpl McMinn was magnificent.

As it began to get light I noticed what looked like 2 white flags waving further down the ridge to the west. Soon about 10 Germans came in – miserable looking creatures, who yielded more loot! These said there were no mines between us and Casa Budriolo and to test this I sent them on their own with a stretcher and a wounded German back to Tac. They didn't blow up!

2 more Germans joined them en route much to our disgust as we weren't able to loot them…

They all arrived safely at Tac…

5 December 1944 (Tuesday)
Spent day improving our positions. There was a thick mist most of the time which enabled us to search some German dug outs on forward slope and got quite a lot of useful stuff. Now and again we got mortared pretty accurately, but luckily had no casualties.

We only had our 'Battle ration' to eat all day (1 tin bully beef and a packet of biscuits), and only the water in our water bottles.

Col Bob came up to see us and I got him to arrange for some bee-hive mines to be put in front of our position that night by the REs.

A very heavy mortar stonk about mid-day, one bomb landed on the rock above my slit trench! L/Sgt Dudgeon did a patrol in the mist towards Pt 313 and shot an unwary German who chose to run away rather than to be taken prisoner! I expected another counter attack during the night, but all was quiet except that L/Cpl O'Connor was hit in the head by Spandau bullets firing on fixed line as he was on sentry on the top of Pt 411.

Food, ammo, water and blankets came up during the night. The latter not until about 0230hrs in the morning by which time we were all bitterly cold. It was a dark & foggy night and I was much relieved when the mines had been laid and all rations etc had come up.

Got a little sleep towards morning. Men all in good spirits, but I pointed out to Col Bob very firmly that I thought we ought to be relieved tomorrow night.

Major the Earl of Lindsay, IRTD, Central Mediterranean Force,   *8 Dec 44*

Of the five young officers who came out, only Colquhoun has gone forward. I saw David Tylden-Wright in Naples yesterday and he should be with you very shortly. Bobby Fisher (GrenadierGuards) who acts as Brigade Liaison Officer between CRU, Brigades and us, has just been down here, but had no particular news of the Battalion except that Colin Dalrymple is now fit and that Freddie Fermor-Hesketh has fallen down a drain in Florence and broken his leg.

John Inskip and CSM Young were both badly wounded but it is hoped that they will pull through. I understand that Inskip has a fracture of the frontal bone of his forehead and the CSM Young lost a hand and has other injuries including a broken leg and damage to one eye.

Charles Whitehead said goodbye to us today but there is no sign of Tom Bland who should be joining him. Perhaps he is not calling here.

Letter from Major R.L. Coke MC, 'S' Coy att C.G.   *15 Dec 44*

I can't remember when I last wrote to you, it seems months ago in view of events here.

.........after a charming spell of 21 days bloodiness including a full scale attack by the Company at the end of it. We had two men killed by a direct hit with a mortar bomb in their trench during our spell of holding a particularly nasty bit of the front. This occurred 26 Nov. We were lucky not to have more casualties there as it was a tricky place with a lot of shelling and mortaring. We caught four Germans prisoners during this period.

On night of Dec 4-5th this Company was ordered to attack a feature called Penzola with the two C.G. Companies acting more or less as flank guards. It was the dominating feature in the German defence line and had to be taken at all costs for some reason. It was a nasty rocky feature about 400 yards long with a peak in the middle a good deal higher than the rest (411 metres). The side facing us, ie South, was practically perpendicular, so we had to go round more or less unknown and unseen country and attack it from the North or German side where it was not so steep. It was a somewhat tricky business and bristled with awful possibilities. Luckily we had very considerable artillery support and POWs after said it was the worse shelling they'd ever had except for one in Russia.

We captured the feature and some 26 POWs including their Company Commander and killed a few others. The Germans counter-attacked later and so we killed a few more. Total casualties that night – two killed and thirteen wounded, which was far less that I had expected and was largely due to the fact that the Germans were at the bottom of their dugouts and had no efficient sentries. POWs said that the first they knew of the attack was when one of their number came and told them that 'The Tommies were on the summit of the hill'.

This rather damped their spirits and most of them didn't show much fight after they realised we held the top. They also expressed great surprise in the attack coming from the north.

The German officer was a brave man and was responsible for shooting poor John Inskip and Guardsman Rush in the right arm with his pistol. This made Guardsman Rush very angry and he changed his TSMG to his left hand and the German Officer duly paid the price with the contents of a magazine in both his legs. He is, as far as I know, still alive but in a pretty bad way.

The attack went in on the hill summit with 9 Platoon (John Inskip) directed on to the top at about 23.30hrs. The badly wounded including poor John had a dreadful time as there was a 'schu' minefield across the only possible route for stretchers back to the RAP and we had to wait until a path had been cleared through it. This was found to be impossible owing to German shelling and mortaring and eventually about 0400 hrs next morning another way was found which entailed getting the stretchers down the almost perpendicular cliff face. This was somehow accomplished without anyone breaking their necks, mainly due to the brilliant work of L/Cpl McMinn, my L/Corporal Stretcher Bearer, although everyone was dead tired with the fighting and approach march over very rough country and L/Cpl McMinn and other stretcher bearers had already had to deal with casualties from a unlucky German DF which caught a few men before we reached the hill. It was pretty cold for the wounded. The POWs, of course, carried the stretchers back. The Company held the hill for two days before being relieved.

Both John and CSM Young are going to be a terrible loss to this Company. John had proved himself a first class Officer and Pln. Comdr. and CSM Young besides being a most charming man, was also the best CSM I have ever served with.

CSM Young was wounded during the counter attack by a German rifle grenade which burst almost on him. He lost his right hand and had a good many other serious injuries I am afraid, including his ear drums blown out. Poor fellow, he was wonderfully brave and cheerful and I hear from hospital he was in that he was doing extraordinarily well. He was quickly sent right back, by aeroplane I think, so don't know where he may be now.

John's bullet went in about the top of his nose and came out through his left eye. I saw him in hospital at Arezzo yesterday. He is doing very well and is already able to get up and walk about. The doctor is very pleased with him and seems fairly confident that there are no other serious injuries other than to his eye. He expects to keep him at Arezzo for 10 days before sending him on to Naples and then home. He was extraordinarily cheerful. I also saw Sacha Carnegie there, who as no doubt you know, was wounded in the cheek, though nothing serious. He too was quite happy and cheerful. I have not been able to see any of my other men as they have all gone right back.

In the attack Ian Fraser and Sgt. McPhail MM were commanding the platoons. Jock Blackett-Ord has gone to 1 S.G. to command 'C' Company, I believe.

I understand there are four Subalterns at IRTD just come out and hope to get one of these shortly. Hope to get some other rank reinforcements.

A letter arrived the other day from Armed Forces Headquarters asking for suggestions for improving morale of troops. It was too good a chance to miss and we had great fun concocting a letter*, of which I will send you a copy as perhaps the Lieutenant-Colonel might be interested to see it!

*See Appendix I

CHAPTER 9

Monte Verro and winter in the mountains

'S' Company enjoyed life at Strada for eight days, during which time it became generally known that all hopes of reaching the Lombardy Plain before the Spring had been officially abandoned. As with the First Battalion Scots Guards in the Monte Sole area, so with the First Guards Brigade's sector in front of Castel del Rio, it was from now on to be a case of frequent and arduous trips into the same piece of the line, interspersed with brief periods of rest in a back area.

The first of these visits began on 20 December when 'S' Company went forward under command of Captain Dalrymple who had returned from hospital only a week before and taken over from Major Coke who had gone off to Rome for a spell of well earned leave. The journey over the mountains took six hours, at the end of which the Company spent the night in the battered village of Fontanelice and moved up on to the slopes of Monte del Verro, next to their old friend Monte dell 'Acqua Salata, on the following day. Owing to casualties and sickness, Captain Dalrymple had only two Scots Guards platoons with him, commanded by Lieutenants Fraser and Wilson, and the Company was made up to strength by the inclusion of a Coldstream platoon under Lieutenant G.V.F. Le Fanu, although little was in fact seen of them as they were almost immediately taken away and placed under command of a forward company. At first 'S' Company were in reserve on a hill called Monte Pieve, where they had the animal quarters of three houses in which to live, one for each platoon and the third for Company Headquarters. No sooner were they thus established, than the weather turned rapidly colder and four inches of snow fell during the first night. This had its advantages as the mud froze and walking became much easier until a sudden thaw made matters far worse than they had ever been before.

Apart from sporadic shelling and the appearance of a solitary German patrol, life was very quiet on Monte Verro and the Company snipers had some good practice picking off the few sheep which wandered unattended across the mountain side and the cooks made swift use of their marksmanship to supplement the monotonous Compo rations – particularly on Christmas Day. According to the Battalion War Diary: 'conditions were worse than before, mud deeper, paths almost non-existent and many dug-outs fallen in'; but this referred mainly to the forward areas and 'S' Company in their houses were luckier. However, on the evening of Boxing Day the Welsh Guards came to take over the area and although the Second Coldstream went back to Strada, 'S' Company, who were considered to have been living in luxury, were kept up at the front the four days they were away, living in comfortable billets in Fontanelice. When they returned on the last day of the year 'S' Company were sent out to forward positions on the mountain where there were no houses, but only small dug-outs and the Company consoled themselves with the fact that, although not so warm as their pig-sties, they were at least not so verminous.

There were now two Coldstream platoons under command and 'S' Company was disposed with two platoons forward on the slope of one hill and the remainder four hundred yards back on the similar slope of another. The nearest enemy positions were about a quarter of a mile away and anyone who looked over the forward crest by day was liable to be shot at. Since, however, it was too cold to leave men out all day in slits from which they could not move without drawing fire, the existing positions just below the crests were taken over as they were found, and each slit provided with a liberal supply of grenades to throw over the sky-line if anything suspicious was heard. The Germans heralded the New Year with a magnificent fireworks display which lasted for about 10 minutes and must have used up much useful ammunition. Nothing else disturbed the quiet on the Battalion front until the evening of 2 January, when the two forward platoons of 'S' Company were attacked by infantry. One of these platoons was a Coldstream one, commanded by Lieutenant D.W. Shenton, and the other was Lieutenant Wilson's; their first indication of impending trouble being a sudden smother of mortar bombs, shells and 28 cm. rockets.

Some days later, a deserter reported that the enemy had, in fact, lost 10 men in this attack but that they had achieved their object. Apparently, or so he said, it had been a straight forward, if expensive, raid in platoon strength to secure an identification; and, when all was over, it was quite true that two Coldstreamers had been found to be missing from the forward positions on 'S' Company's left. The battle had only lasted for about fifteen minutes, but for the forward sections and in particular that protecting the left flank which was commanded by Lance Corporal Heap, it had been fast and furious. Under cover of the shelling, a strong force of Germans had managed to approach his position in the darkness and to lie up in dead ground only a few yards from his forward slit trenches. Immediately the barrage had lifted on to the next crest, these Germans had charged over the sky-line, firing their automatic weapons from the hip and throwing grenades. Gallant though they were, they had not bargained on meeting Heap, who jumped swiftly out of his trench as they rushed forward and, also firing from the hip, chased them smartly back the way they had come. Disregarding the continuous fire from a flank, he then returned to his men and went to each slit trench, issuing more grenades and giving encouragement, although wounded by a bullet before he was half way round. Twice more the enemy attacked his position and each time they were flung back with losses. Throughout the night, whilst more attacks were expected, Lance Corporal Heap remained with his section, refusing to be evacuated until it became light. For such gallantry he was later awarded a Military Medal.

After this brief but exciting interlude, the rest of the Company's spell in the line was uneventful and on 6 January the Battalion made its way back down the well worn paths in pitch darkness and pouring rain and returned to Strada by truck. And so it went on. Four more times 'S' Company returned to Monte del Verro, but never again to such excitement.

Lieutenant P.H. Bartholomew had by now joined the Company as replacement for Lieutenant Inskip and CSM Taylor from the First Battalion was well established in place of CSM Young. The Company were grieved to hear, however, that the latter's wounds had now caused him to lose his right foot, in addition to the hand which had been blown off on Monte Penzola, but that he was at home in a hospital in England and, as usual, extremely cheerful. Major Coke, Captain Dalrymple and Lieutenants Wilson and Fraser all remained with the Company through the dreary Winter weeks and were with it when, on 14 February the Battalion marched off the sodden and thawed-out Monte Verro for the last time and drove down the long, twisting and all too familiar mountain road through Castel del Rio and Firenzuola to the billet area at Strada. One week later, they were on their way even further South to Spoleto, only sixty miles from Rome, and passing through country over which they had fought during the heat of the previous Summer. Four days before them, 24th Guards Brigade with the First Battalion of the Regiment had made the very same southward journey from the Setta valley, and at Spoleto the two Brigades met.

Maj R.L.Coke MC   *'S' Coy att. C.G.*   *17 Jan 45*

We got out of the line again back here yesterday morning after a shorter spell than usual, only 6 days! But that is quite long enough under the weather conditions now prevailing up there. There is about 2ft of snow in the ruts and the tracks are frozen and like glass. It took us four hours from leaving our positions to reach the road, during which each one of us fell at least a hundred times and did a fair part of the way on our behinds! It took a further 8 hrs in TCVs to get back here and a very perilous journey over the slippery roads down the steep hill from the pass! We had a very quiet time as far as the Germans were concerned, which was a good job – no doubt they were chiefly occupied in keeping themselves warm. We've got proper mountain equipment now, which is excellent, but still the same ammunition boots which are quite useless and leak like sieves, so no one ever has dry feet. Peter Bartholomew, our new Officer was in action for the first time and I think he will turn out well.

I believe Colin Dalrymple wrote and told you about the time before in the line when he was commanding (I was on leave) and the company beat off an attack with pretty heavy losses to the Germans at no cost to 'S' Company. Italian civilians whom we got information from this time said the Germans had a lot killed and wounded, which is all to the good.

Some decorations for this Company have just come through this moment. They are:- L/Corporal McMinn and Gdsn Rush MMs. I hope there will be some others too, but no more through yet. All are very well deserved.

NOTE:- Maj R.L. Coke MC has been awarded the DSO

Captain The Hon C.J. Dalrymple.   *'S' Coy att C.G.*   *21 Jan 45*

Richard told me to write to you some days ago, to account for the merry Christmas spent by 'S' Company but I am afraid I have been slow in starting. We left our billet area near Florence at 0500 hrs on 20 Dec and drove for six hours, crossing the mountains and eventually arriving in the area we know pretty well. There was a change of plan at the last moment so we spent the night in a most battered village called Fontanelice and moved up the hill the following day. We were reserve company on a hill called Monte Pieve, where we had three houses to live in; one for each platoon and one for Coy H.Q. I should have mentioned that the company consisted of No 7 Platoon with Ian Fraser, 8 Platoon with Jim Wilson and a Coldstream Platoon, whose officer was Victor Le Fanu, but they were under the command of a forward company and had no more dealings with us. The march up the hill was most unpleasant. The mud churned up by the mules often let one in up to the knees and then held firmly to one's feet. The houses were mostly demolished but the pigsties or animal accommodation was in fact underneath so we lived there. Quite revolting but safe. The supply of candles is entirely inadequate, so we used cigarette tin lamps filled with petrol, the smoke from which contributed largely to the dirt. Previous occupants had not taken the problem of sanitation too seriously; there were piles of empty tins everywhere, no latrines and two bodies within fifteen yards of Ian's house. Presumably the excuse for leaving them had been the fact that they were on a forward slope but we took advantage of a misty day to cover them

97

in.The weather turned rapidly colder and about four inches of snow fell the first day; however it has its advantages for the mud froze and walking became less laborious. A few shells landed on the forward companies and there was one German patrol but nothing to upset us. There were a few sheep wandering about unattended so we did well as regards food, particularly on Christmas Day; good practice for the snipers and a welcome supplement to our company rations.

We were relieved by a Welsh Guards Company on the night of the 26 December, when the rest of the Battalion came all the way back to Florence. Having been in reserve though we were kept in comfortable billets in Fontanelice in case Brigade wanted to send patrols to a certain area in the valley to the north. We did not have to do any and remained in reasonable comfort until the night of the 31 December, when the whole Battalion returned and we were sent to a forward position holding Ponte del Verro.

This time we had no houses and lived in very small dug-outs, which I found much warmer and, so long as they continued to be dry, in most ways preferable. We had two Coldstream platoons under command and were disposed with two forward on the reverse slope of one hill and the rest of us 400 yards back on a second and very similar one. The nearest enemy positions were about 400 yards away and all movement by day had to be confined to small areas. The forward position presented certain obvious difficulties because of a very sharp hill crest. Any one who looked over by day got shot at and we could not find places to dig on the forward slope by night. It is too cold to leave men all day in a slit trench from which they cannot get out. Accordingly we accepted the place as it already was, with slits behind the crest and a good supply of grenades to chuck over if anything was heard.

All went well until the night of the 2 January when forward platoons (Jim Wilson and David Shenton Coldstream Guards) were attacked at 1930hrs. We were unloading the mules at Coy H.Q. at the time when an extremely large shower of shells arrived. Our hill was steep so most of them hit the top or burst well behind us but it could hardly have been more unpleasant and every single telephone line was cut. After perhaps a minute, a stream of tracer was fired over us, which I thought was probably giving direction, so I ran to my dug-out and eventually got through to Bn H.Q. on the wireless to call down the DFs which appeared suitable. Fortunately the same conclusion had been reached further back and the gunners had already begun. The wireless sets all worked and after a time Jim Wilson came up on the air and said that three lots of Germans had appeared on his hill top, had thrown lots of stick grenades but had been met with the appropriate fashion and all his positions were intact. He thought they had accounted for at least 10 and that as our shelling was landing very thick in front, they had probably lost a good many people. We consequently continued it for the benefit of any others who might still be lying out there.

After a bit we took a carrying party forward with more grenades and ammunition. One Coldstreamer was moderately wounded and had to be carried away. One German was semi-conscious and later died in hospital, a second was dead on the hill, L/Corporal Heap was cut in one hand but was not evacuated until the next night. Two Coldstreamers had been removed from one of the slits on the top of the hill and have not reappeared. Their journey to the enemy lines through the DFs

98

can hardly have been much fun. It was hard to tell whether we were being attacked by a fighting patrol or something more substantial, but the fact that they made three attempts to get our hill seems to indicate that they wanted more than their two prisoners and intended to stay. We have not been able to go out and search for bodies since but some Italians told a patrol that they had had lots killed and wounded so one hopes that they did.

As a final effort they fired five very large rockets at us, which started their flight with a remarkably unpleasant noise and landed with an equally nasty bang. The rest of our spell in the line was uneventful. It took four hours in pitch darkness and heavy rain to march down to the transport on the night of 6 Jan. We got to the embussing point at 0100 hrs – soaked – and back to Florence at 0815hrs on 7 Jan 45.

Since then they have done one more spell of five days in and are now doing another, Richard (Coke) commanding in each case. The only casualty is one man burnt by a petrol burner. There is lots of fresh snow.

CHAPTER 10

The Last Parade and Reorganization at Spoleto – February/March 1945

After the gruelling time spent in the harsh winter months of 1944 and early 1945, 1st Guards Brigade had rested at Strada, south of Florence. This area was well known to them as they had spent time at R. & R. here during their many battles in the mountains.

This last week was spent getting cleaned up and making final preparations for the journey to Spoleto where both the 1st Guards Brigade and 24 Guards Brigade were to meet and reorganise. Prior to all this, there was a Farewell Parade before General Murray, who bade a fond farewell to the 2nd Bn. Coldstream Guards on behalf of 6th Armoured Division. The days were almost up for the 'S' Company attachment and it was relatively clear that the whole company would be transferred to 1st Battalion Scots Guards.

The parade was in two parts, the inspection by Colonel Coates, followed by

Spoleto Castle 2003

the inspection of General Murray. After the General had spoken to them and brought out the fact that Penzola was a very fine performance, 'S' Company marched past the rest of the Coldstream, who presented arms as 'S' Company gave them an eyes left. The pipes played the Company March, the 79th Farewell to Gibraltar, as they marched down the road to the General and gave him an eyes left too.

For the Second Coldstream, this meeting with their Third Battalion meant the same major re-shuffle as had occurred when the First and Second Battalion Scots Guards had met at Sorrento twelve months before. On this occasion, it was the Third Battalion who were to sail for Home and the Second who were to be made up to strength to carry on the struggle. For the first time in a year there were plenty of Coldstreamers to go round and the days of the 'S' Company attachment were obviously numbered. Not surprisingly the First Battalion Scots Guards welcomed this situation with outstretched arms. It is a strange man who is not pleased to rejoin a Battalion of his own Regiment, and 'S' Company were naturally delighted to go to the First Battalion; but at the same time, there was little doubt that they were extremely sad to be leaving their Coldstream comrades with whom they had been so happy and in whose company they had achieved so much. For their part, the Second Coldstream were kind enough to say that they were sorry too, and Colonel Coates, under whose command 'S' Company had served for the major part of their attachment, presented to each man a handsome card with an inscription which ran as follows: 'In appreciation of the excellent fighting spirit and splendid record of 'S' Company and in remembrance of those who have fallen whilst fighting with the Second Battalion Coldstream Guards'. The names of the eight major engagements with which 'S' Company had been associated (Cassino, Monte Piccolo, Perugia, Monte Lignano, Advance to the Gothic Line, Gothic Line, Monte Battaglia and Monte Penzola); the two Regimental stars and a list of those in the Company to whom decorations had been awarded (2 DSOs, one Military Cross, two Distinguished Service Medals, and nine Military Medals – a 10th was awarded after the cards had been printed) completed a souvenir of twelve months' comradeship which will always find an honoured place amongst the treasures of those who were fortunate enough to receive one.

On 1 March 'S' Company officially ceased to be and were posted to their new Battalion in whose ranks they took their place, complete and without re-organisation, as 'B' Company, First Battalion Scots Guards.

Having met at Spoleto, the final re-organisation took place as follows:-

1st Guards Brigade – Brigadier G.L. Verney – still in 6th Armoured Division.
   3rd Bn. Grenadier Guards
   1st Bn. Welsh Guards
   1st Bn. The Welch Regiment

24 Guards Brigade – Brigadier M.D. Erskine DSO – transferred to the 56 (London) Division (Major General J.Y. Whitfield).
   2nd Bn. Coldstream Guards
   1st Bn. Scots Guards
   1st Bn. The Buffs
The Commanding Officer of 1st Bn. Scots Guards, which 'S' Company joined as 'B' Company, was Lieutenant Col. R.G. Lewthwaite MC

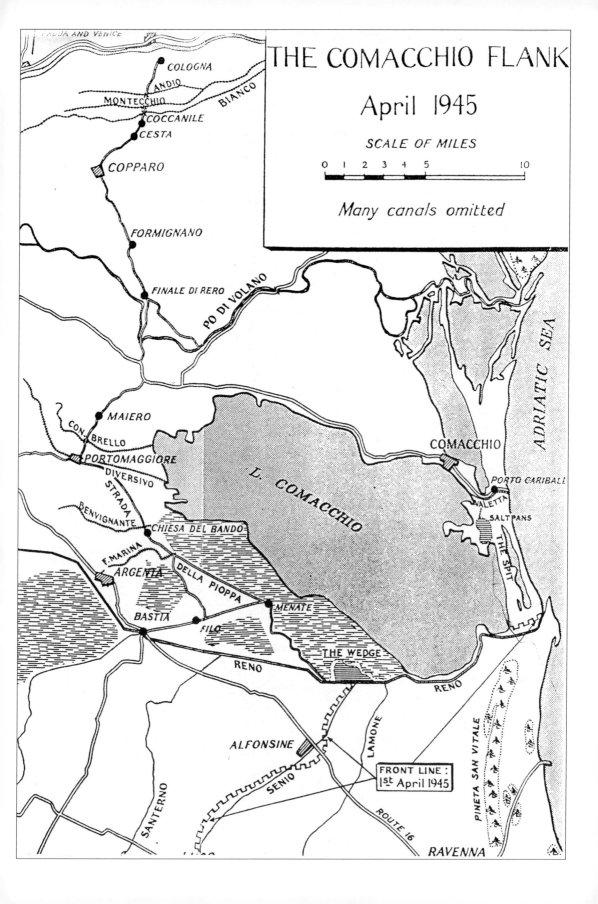

THE COMACCHIO FLANK

April 1945

SCALE OF MILES

0 1 2 3 4 5   10

Many canals omitted

COLOGNA

ANDIO

MONTECCHIO

BIANCO

COCCANILE

CESTA

COPPARO

FORMIGNANO

FINALE DI RERO

PO DI VOLANO

ADRIATIC SEA

MAIERO

CON. BRELLO

PORTOMAGGIORE

DIVERSIVO

STRADA

BENVIGNANTE

CHIESA DEL BANDO

L. COMACCHIO

COMACCHIO

PORTO CARIBALL

VALETTA

SALTPANS

THE SPIT

F. MARINA

ARGENTA

DELLA PIOPPA

BASTIA

MENATE

FILO

THE WEDGE

RENO

RENO

ALFONSINE

LAMONE

PINETA SAN VITALE

FRONT LINE:
1st April 1945

SANTERNO

SENIO

ROUTE 16

RAVENNA

CHAPTER 11

Comacchio – Argenta – The PO

'S' Company now serving as 'B' Company 1st Battalion Scots Guards

After a period of some 4 weeks spent at Spoleto, the Battalion embussed in TCVs on 10 March and passed through the mountains travelling northwards through Fano and on to Forli. Here 24 Guards Brigade joined 56th (London) Division and changed their shoulder badges from the yellow and green triangle of the South African Division to the Black Cat. Intensive training took place in preparation for the next offensive – this included training with Kangaroo troop carriers. The Battalion made a good initial impression in sporting activity by winning both the Association and Rugby football championships in the Division.

The pine woods at Ravenna 2003

Before leaving Forli, the Battalion managed to thwart a bad inspection report by the Inspector of Army Equipment. This was achieved by good luck, as 2nd Battalion Coldstream Guards were visited first. While this inspection was going on, the Scots Guardsmen secreted excess jeeps and stores away into the hills. After the Inspectors' departure, the stores returned and life went on as usual!

On 1 April, the Battalion moved quietly out of Forli and headed towards the pine woods at Ravenna. They trained here, using the newly arrived Buffaloes, renamed Fantails, which were amphibious vehicles designed to cross the Pacific breakers. The actual usefulness of these amphibious tractors had yet to be tested on the marsh and mud of North East Italy. The front line at this stage ran roughly along the banks of the River Senio to the point where it ran into the marshes at a feature called the Wedge, on the southern banks of Lake Comacchio.

Two amphibious operations were required to clear the way for the main Eighth Army attack. The first was the capture of a feature called the Spit, a strip of sandy land which separated Lake Comacchio from the sea. The second was known as the Wedge, which was the flooded fields and dykes north of the River Reno. The seizure of the Spit was placed in the hands of 2 Commando Brigade and 24 Guards Brigade and was designed to draw down enemy reserves to this sector. The second operation – to capture the Wedge – was designed to provide a springboard for further advances to the North West.

Activities in the Po Valley were complex to say the least and to get a complete picture of the progress of 'B' Company it makes eminently better reading to insert here Major Richard Coke's diary from 20 March 1945 to 30 April 1945:

Extract from Major Richard Coke's Diary

20 March 1945 (Tuesday)
Early start this morning. The Company left Forli at 0730 hrs to practise with the kangaroos (Sherman tanks with the turret removed).

The 8th Army Commander General McCreery, came to see us about lunch time with the Div Commander and the Brigadier.

It was a very hot day & we were in shirt sleeves order. After lunch we did a demonstration for all officers and NCOs in the Battalion. This included mounting & dismounting drill & a platoon attack on a house done by Ian Fraser's platoon (10 Platoon).

The men enjoyed rushing round in kangaroos. We got one ditched in a dyke, as Colin more or less dared the little officer to try & get one across it. It had to be pulled out.

The Coldstream had three men killed & others badly injured when one of their kangaroos blew up on a mine. I am afraid that it is inevitable that this will happen in this area. Why couldn't they have left us at Spoleto...

We had dinner tonight & a bad piper (Findlayson). I asked Peter St Juste (Italian Liaison Officer at Bde HQ to dine & Col Barne (Nigel's brother, who commands 4th Hussar) came. He looks very like Nigel.

Michael Barne is 2 i/c at Pirbright. Col John Dalyrmple is going home to command Training Battalion.

Had charming letters from Hugh Kindersley, who got wounded about D day & has been in hospital for 9 months, & also Joe Airlie who says his son David has just joined the regiment.

21 March 1945 (Wednesday)
Spent all day on the field firing range, where we fired a lot of ammo.

Heard from Gioia, who said F.M. Alex had called to see Aunt Bea & had tea at the flat, also Desmond Chichester.

I am so glad as now perhaps he will be able to do something to help them. Gioia had met Jim Eagan & he was going to take her back to Madaloni.

22 March 1945 (Thursday)
Lovely day.

Mar 23rd 1945 (Friday)
Had a letter from Uncle Barney. The Div Commander spoke to all officers in the division and gave us lunch afterwards. Saw Charles Mitchell, Jock B-Ord's brother in law.

24 March 1945 (Saturday)
Battalion Kangaroo exercise. 'B' Company acted as enemy. Very hot. I was an umpire & wandered around, principally watching George Mann with RE.

Had a long talk with Col Tony Barne who commands 4th Hussars & is a brother of Michael. He told me he had been abroad for six and half years & in all done 17 years abroad.

Exercise ended about 3 p m. After tea Tommy Bulkeley & I went off to stay with Col Freddie Shrimpton at Corvia. He gave us a good dinner & a cigar.

Heard something of future operations. Hope the war ends before we have to do our stuff!

25 March 1945 (Sunday)
Rather a hang-over from last night.

Got up at 0500 hrs. Met the Town Major in the square at Cervia at 0600 hrs. & we went out shooting. The guns were Col Freddie, Bill, his 2 i/c, Town Major, Tommy & I. We had great fun. I borrowed David Toler's gun. We got 13 duck including 2 Shovellers, mostly teal, 1 curlew, 1 snipe, 2 various. I shot 6 teal (includg 2 rt. & lefts) the curlew, snipe & the 2 various, which were sandpipers or knots -v. good to eat. I missed one very easy duck which was annoying. There were a lot of duck about, but of course the place is shot night & day nonstop. Got back about 10 a m, had a bath & changed & then attended cocktail party which was fun. Returned Forli after lunch. We arranged another shoot on Wednesday.

26 March 1945 (Monday)
Street fighting after lunch in a little village E of Cesena.

The trouble is that all the inhabitants have returned to it + belongings, which makes it a little difficult to practise realistically!

We let off some 'beehives' & pole charges against a wall & practised the drill for clearing a house.

Col Ray came and watched & to my surprise seemed quite pleased! Col John Dalrymple came too to say good-bye to the Battalion as he is going home to command Training Battalion. He saw through our training all right!

Col Johnny Bland & Col John Dalrymple came to dinner.

Offensive in Germany going marvellously well. Everyone here is rather wondering whether the war will be over before we have to start our offensive here. I doubt it! The suspense is rather awful.

27 March 1945 (Tuesday)
Company practised river-crossing in assault boats and laying kapok bridging across the Mentone R. which runs through Forli.

It is only about 25 ft wide, but better than nothing.

28 March 1945 (Wednesday)
TEWT for all officers on Night Attack set by Tommy Bulkeley. It was well done & quite interesting. We spent most of the day out on the ground in the old Poggioli castle area.

After tea David Malcolm, Colin Dalrymple & I went over to shoot at Cervia. We met Col Freddie Shrimpton, who was the only one who could come, in the market place at 5:15 p m.

The total bag was 8 teal, probably garganey. There were a lot of duck in the air at one time, but they soon cleared off & did not come back.

Freddie S got hopelessly stuck in the mud for about 10 mins & eventually had to get out of his gum boots & walk to the car in his bare feet!

I only got 1 teal. Colin had a good shoot & got 5.

We had dinner afterwards with Col F.

He thought that we were being kept for exploitation in the coming attack, which was due to start about 31st.

29 March 1945 (Thursday)
Battalion night exercise, which lasted until 0800 hrs 30th. It might have been worse.

After our Company attack which ended about mid-night, we ate cold teal in a farm-house & I went to sleep on some flour sacks for 2 or 3 hrs.

30 March 1945 (Friday) Good Friday

News this morning was that Americans had pushed a further 50 miles E of Rhine yesterday & not much organised resistance.

Col Ray had an 0 Gp at 1800 hrs. in which he told us we would move to a concentration area N of Ravenna on Sunday & practice in 'Fantails' on the way.

24th Guards Brigade is to be used in the Comacchio peninsula after the Commandos have done their stuff.

Everyone rather hoping that the war in Germany will be over in 3 or 4 days & that then the Germans in Italy will pack up, but I am afraid it looks as if we shall be in for one more battle before that happens!

31 March 1945 (Saturday)

Preparing for move! I told the Coy about it at mid-day. Morale seems very high.

We eat the remaining teal for dinner.

Had an amusing letter from Hugo Charteris to say that he was at Caterham & had been in trouble with the Maj-General over something he had written to Sir Edward Grigg about a remark that gentleman had made about tanks!

APRIL

1 April 1945 (Sunday) Easter Sunday

Left Forli 0800 hrs with L.F. (Tony Tuke) to train in 'Fantails' at a place on the coast E. of Ravenna.

They seemed pretty good things (amphibious tracked vehicles), but the RASC who drive them want a lot of training as to how to land troops.

They would insist on landing both companies on a stretch of beach about 100 yards long. A lovely hot day.

Colin went off early with a small party to recce our concentration area about 3 miles from the front lines and S. of the Commachio Isthmus.

Colin joined us about mid-day. We were supposed to move to the concentration area about 2 p m, but this was wisely put off until after dark, so the whole Company had to stay where we were until about 7.20 p.m.

Colin, Ian & I went off in the jeep to Cervia & had tea in the British Red Cross officers' convalescent home with Eve Hinde, who runs it, & used to be at the one at Sorrento. General McLeod who runs the British Red Cross was there too & seemed a nice old boy, though a bit dull.

We arrived in concentration area without incident at about 9.30 p m & got safely dug in.

Col Ray told us that 3 Commandos were being landed at various places on the Isthmus during the course of the night, & that Freddie Shrimpton's battery of M 10s would probably go off. They will fire directly over our heads & about 100 yards behind us! In fact they didn't fire until about 0400 hrs., when they let off a good stonk & woke us all up!

A Happy Easter!

Put the clocks forward 1 hr. tonight to double British Summer time.

2 April 1945 (Monday)

All day in concentration area. We were at 2 hrs. notice to move, but this never materialised & we spent a quiet night. Col Ray had an 0 gp at 0900 hrs. at which he insisted that I should be LOB & that Colin should command.

The Commando landings last night went very well after a shaky start, and by nightfall the Commandos had taken over 400 POWs & reached as far as the 1st big canal across the isthmus. This is about 4000 yards N. of the R.Reno, which up to now had been the front line.

The fantails which were used for 1 Commando proved rather a failure, as they all got stuck on the sandbanks in the lake & instead of landing at midnight, did not land until 0700 hrs this morning.

Had a drink with Freddie Shrimpton whose HQ is just behind BN HQ. Area is a good one, very sandy soil with strips of young pine trees about 10 ft high which give good cover. Tommy Bulkeley discovered some duck in a marsh, just next door to us, which I hope the 'A' echelon personnel will have time to go after. Apparently the Comacchio lake area used to be a very good duck shoot in peace-time.

6th Guards Tank Brigade (includg 3rd Battalion Scots Guards) were mentioned on BBC as 'Battling' a way into Munster to day.

3 April 1945 (Tuesday) My birthday (27)

Spent all day in the same area & another quiet night with no move.

The Commandos by nightfall had pushed up to the line of the Barletta Canal without much opposition.

No doubt 24th Guards Brigade will take over from them there, & have the sticky task of getting over the canal & getting Comacchio!

Borrowed L/Cpl Moore's old hammer gun & went to the marsh next to us with Tommy B. for the evening flight. The old gun had no fore-end, so I had to take a ram rod to eject the empty cases. 2 young Italians came with us & towed us out to 2 good hides (dry barrels sunk in the mud), but we saw no duck & never fired a shot. They are keen that we should go after snipe with them sometime tomorrow, but we shall have to see what the situation is & how the battle is going by then.

Had a letter from Aunt Mabel asking me if I would like to have Uncle Ned's gun. It was made for him by Boss & had never been used. His own pair had been bombed in London early in the war. Naturally I accepted!

Col Freddie Shrimpton went off today to fly home for 3 weeks leave under LIAP. I went & had a drink with him at lunch time.

4 April 1945 (Wednesday)

The Battalion moved up about mid-day to another concentration area North of Bellocchio. 'B' Company under Colin. The LOBs (about 18 from 'B' Company) stayed in the same area.

The Battalion, were very nearly made to attack across the Barletta canal tonight, much to their dismay, but fortunately this was put off. In the end 'B' & 'C' Companies relieved the Commandos and RF & LF were kept in reserve.

I went up about 7 pm with Tommy Bulkeley to see how things were going. The Company had already moved off so did not see them.

Saw some of the commandos who reckoned they'd killed a good many Germans & done for about 1000 in all including about 800 prisoners. They'd had some casualties themselves. However they've done well.

I hope we don't have to cross the Barletta canal. I fear it might be a very sticky proceeding.

The Germans weren't shelling the road, much to my surprise. God knows why not as there was masses of transport on it, & a few shells would have created chaos.

Tommy & I got back about mid-night.

5 April 1945 (Thursday)

The Battalion were ordered to make a feint attack across the Barletta Canal, & if not much opposition to make a bridge head the other side.

The plan roughly is for LF to cross with RE in reserve ready to cross after them. 'B' Company hold their positions. I thought it sounded a very risky plan & we stand to lose a lot of casualties unless either (a) The Germans have cleared out - most unlikely or (b) they surrender without a fight!

Went to bed about 9 pm most unhappy about it all.

167 Brigade (London Scottish, London Irish & a Battalion of Royal Fusiliers) attacked tonight across the Reno westwards of the lake. I listened to the artillery barrage for them from my camp bed. It was a very considerable one & went on for about one and a half hrs. I was very glad I was in bed!

6 April 1945 (Friday)

Heard at breakfast that the Battalion feint attack had met with considerable opposition & a large enemy stonk. Poor Angus Colquhoun & a guardsman with him were the first to cross the canal in a recce boat!! God knows why they didn't swim! They got three quarters of the way across & were fired on. They are missing but doubtless both are killed; or wounded & drowned. The rest of the Company (LF) did not cross. It was lucky the Germans did not wait to open fire until most of the Company were across, they might have got the lot!

A heavy stonk came down, but luckily only killed 1 full sergeant in LF. George Mann was slightly wounded in the cheek. All 'B' Coy all right fortunately.

A very unnecessary & unfortunate operation ending in the loss of a first class platoon commander & a platoon sergeant.

167 Bde have got across the river all right & are making slow progress.

Col Ray went to IRTD at Fano for 1 night. Tommy went up to command. Kirkham (12 Platoon) got a near miss with a shell on his slit trench which perforated an eardrum.

7 April 1945 (Saturday)

Nothing much doing.

Coldstream lost an officer called Count Bentinck last night trying to cross the canal.

Went to Rear Bde HQ & had tea & supper with Dickie Westmacott.

2nd Battalion Coldstream Guards are likely to come out & 1st Battalion Scots Guards to take over the whole line.

A 45,000 ton Japanese warship, the biggest they've got, has been sunk together with some other Japanese ships in the Pacific.

12 miles from Bremen. News is pretty good, but the war still goes on! Main 8th Army attack is due about 9th I think.

8 April 1945 (Sunday)

Tommy Bulkeley, Tim L. Peto & I went off after lunch to IRTD at Fano. En route we saw George Mann in hospital near Rimini. They've taken a piece of shell splinter out of his cheek & he ought to be back in 2 or 3 weeks.

Found David Cuthbert, Ronnie Rowe, Jock B-Ord, John Pope, David Willis, Bobbie Wells at IRTD. Had an amusing dinner.

9 April 1945 (Monday)

John Pope showed me the war memorial to those killed in 2nd Battalion Coldstream Guards. Col Bob apparently ordered it, unknown to me.

One of the Battalion pioneers carved the star & names very well indeed on a bit of marble, one for Coldstream Guards & one for 'S' Company. Col Bob apparently wants them put in a church in either Florence or Rome. (Note: They are now in the English church in Florence – St. Mark's Church, Via Maggio)

Visited San Marino on the way back to the Battalion. Wonderful view from the top of the rock, but otherwise rather uninteresting! Most of the houses & the wall have been renewed recently in very bad taste. It is quite free from war damage.

Returned to 'B' echelon about 6.30 p m to find that an operation is going on tonight up at the Battalion, in which 'B' Company are to clear the area of some salt-pans at N.W. corner of the spit & S of the canal. I am to go up tomorrow morning in case any re-organisation is needed.

Main 8th Army attack to night across R. Senio. New Zealanders, Poles & 8th Indian Div all attacked & got bridgeheads across.

10 April 1945 (Tuesday)

Went up to the Battalion. 'B' Company near BN HQ in reserve positions.

There had been some trouble last night with 11 Platoon which Colin & Jim were very worried about.

Went into it all with the Commanding Officer very carefully, with the result that L/Sgt Livingstone is now a guardsman & will be transferred to another company.

Jim himself didn't do at all well which is very unlike him & in general 11 Platoon bogged it badly. Had a chance of taking a house with a few prisoners & missed it.

Col. Ray & I both wanted 11 Platoon to do the job again tonight & do it properly; but the whole Battalion is being relieved by A Commando, & so we can't.

The Company got back to the 'B' echelon area about 8 p.m. as it was getting dark.

11 April 1945 (Wednesday)

Spent the day cleaning up etc. We all went & had a mobile bath, which was very necessary, but not very enjoyable!

Cocktail party in the evening. Very strong S.African brandy cocktails. Col Billy Steele there, Billy Gunther, Bill Rosslow & others. Got rather tight.

Went to dinner at the Club Ravenna with Col Billy, Bob Southey, Jamie Leveson & other Coldstream. Col Billy in splendid form.

Poor Bob Southey overturned his jeep on the way back. He had his Medical Officer with him. Both were rather shaken. We got Hugh & the ambulance to go out to them, but apparently they are all right.

Got to bed about midnight.

Big 8th Army attack going well. The New Zealanders have now got a bridgehead over the R.Santerno.

News from Germany is wonderful. Americans advanced 70 miles in 1 day & are now only 70 miles from Berlin! British close to Bremen. Still the war goes on!

24th Gds Bde is to be used in the near future for our attack on Argenta.

12 April 1945 (Thursday)

Rather a hang-over today. Billy Gunther asked me to dine with him tonight but I refused.

'A' Commando & a Parachute Brigade are to help us in the attack on Argenta. We may move tomorrow night.

Went to bed fairly early.

13 April 1945 (Friday)

Woken up at 0600 hrs. Orders to move forward at 0845 to another concentration area at Menate. Went a long way round by San Alberto & Alfonsine. I had to lead the Battalion column in a jeep.

Arrived in concentration area about 12.45 hrs, after very slow progress from Alfonsine onwards owing to traffic jams. etc.

Colin, who left with the Bn advance party at 0600 hrs arrived only an hour or two before us.

All the villages N of R.Reno had been bombed flat.

Pretty heavy fighting seems to be going on, & the Buffs seem to be having a rough time, but news is scanty. 2nd Battalion Coldstream Guards were ahead of us & will no doubt be committed either tonight or tomorrow.

The Commando did not land in the right place, as their fantails could not cross a dyke & had not had much to do up to date. No doubt will be flung in tonight.

Weather holds fine.

Within 50 miles of Berlin now. Leipzig by-passed.

14 April 1945 (Saturday)

Stayed in same area until about tea time, when we got a sudden order to move, after it seemed pretty certain that we should spend another peaceful night!

I had a bad nosebleed just before going off on a recce & didn't feel in my best form.

Met Col Ray at La Prioppa where I found an 0 gp in progress.

The form was that 9 Commando were to try & rush the bridge over the Fossa Marina & capture it intact. 'B' Coy to be under their command to go across & consolidate the other side if they were successful. They had first to clear several groups of houses. S. of the canal known by the code names: Nokes, Oldham & Oppenshaw.

H hr was 2400 hrs. About this time I went up to Commando Tac HQ at 'Flannel' and stayed with their Commanding officer for the rest of the time.

The company had marched up under Jim Wilson to a house just N of La Prioppa. By about 0100 hrs the Commando had taken Nokes, Oldham & Oppenshaw & a SP gun intact. I ordered the Company to move up to Plug in case the bridge should be taken intact, but it was partially blown with a tiger tank at the N end of it. Eventually at about 0400 hrs after a good deal of palaver, the operation was cancelled & the company marched back to our house having had a wretched time waiting about in the cold.

This means that 1st Battalion Scots Guards will have to put in a Battalion attack to cross the canal tomorrow night.

15 April 1945 (Sunday)

I was woken up after only about 1 hr's sleep at 0715 hrs by an irate Brigadier Malcolm Erskine, who accused me of having no sentries & also of not standing to. I was furious & told him that I'd never stood to with my company yet as a regular thing at dawn & had no intention of doing so! A senior NCO later commented: He (the Brigadier) has always been like that'.

We went out & found the double sentry all right, but unfortunately one of the men was smoking, which was not too good!

Got a little sleep until lunch time.

O gp at Bn HQ for the assault across the canal at 1500 hrs.

Very long & complicated orders. 1st Battalion Scots Guards to assault W of the bridge & 9 Commando East. 'B' Company right & 'C' left.

Peter Bartholomew went out at last light (2030 hrs) & had to be back for a conference at 2200 hrs which didn't give him much time.

H hr was 0400 hrs. We moved from our house at 0130 hrs & marched to Boat assembly area behind 'C' Company.

Only 6 assault boats to each company, so only 2 platoons could get across at a time. 12 & 11 (Peter & Jim) to go first followed by 10 (Sgt Parkinson as Ian is LOB)) + Coy HQ.

Boats to be launched in the 2 canals running due N & parallel to each other & both leading into Fossa Marina.

Had a party of 24 men from LF as rowers & boat carriers.

As soon as we tried to launch the boats, we were seen & heavy & accurate machine gun fire & mortar came down. This was 400 yards from the main canal! It was a bright night & the artificial moonlight (searchlights) didn't help matters! In spite of a lot of artillery (3 field & 4 medium regiments) the thing was obviously not on for us.

'C' Coy (David Malcolm) couldn't get their boats anywhere near the canal. Col Ray not very helpful when we told him about it on the wireless. 'C'. Company & the RAP + LF rowers had a few casualties – 'C' Company from shu-mines.

We hung about without being able to get definite orders.

Time was getting short and it was getting light. Eventually we got the order to dig in where we were.

RF + LF (in reserve) were ordered to be ready to support the Commandos if they got across. Eventually just before it got light we were ordered to withdraw & we were lucky to get out & back without further casualties.

The operation might have succeeded in a thick fog, but as it was, it was impossible. Got back to our house about 0800 hrs.

Saw 2nd Battalion Coldstream Guards tac HQ on the way - Col Billy, Mike Hollings & Bob Clive.

16 April 1945 (Monday)
More 0 gp after lunch.

The buildings & N bank of Fossa Marina canal were well bombed & shot up all afternoon by aircraft including mediums.

The plan is for 1st Battalion Scots Guards to relieve the Buffs & Commandos tonight at dusk, & for LF to try & infiltrate over the bridge by the pumping station, which has about a 20 ft gap only blown in it.

If they are successful in forming a small bridgehead, then 'B' Company will go through and take the 'factory square' area.

Had a bit of trouble before the start with 11 Platoon led by one or two old soldiers who said they thought it was a suicide scheme.

Jim Wilson, who does not appear to be himself these days, did little to put things right!

At 2020 hrs I was told about it, & we were due to move off to relieve a Buffs Company on the road about 500 yards from the bridge at 2030hrs.

I had a talk to the whole platoon, & then got rid of Jim Wilson & told L/Sgt Allardyce to command it. Jim Wilson must go back to IRTD or somewhere for a bit until he has regained his confidence.

This left me with only 1 officer, Peter Bartholomew, & 2 full sergeants, 11 Platoon being commanded by L/Sgt Allardyce & 10 Platoon by Sgt Parkinson.

We took over from 1 Buffs without incident, & at about 0330 hrs got the order to move forward as LF had got across the Pumping station, & the gap had been bridged by tying together about 4 or 5 assault boats. A sapper

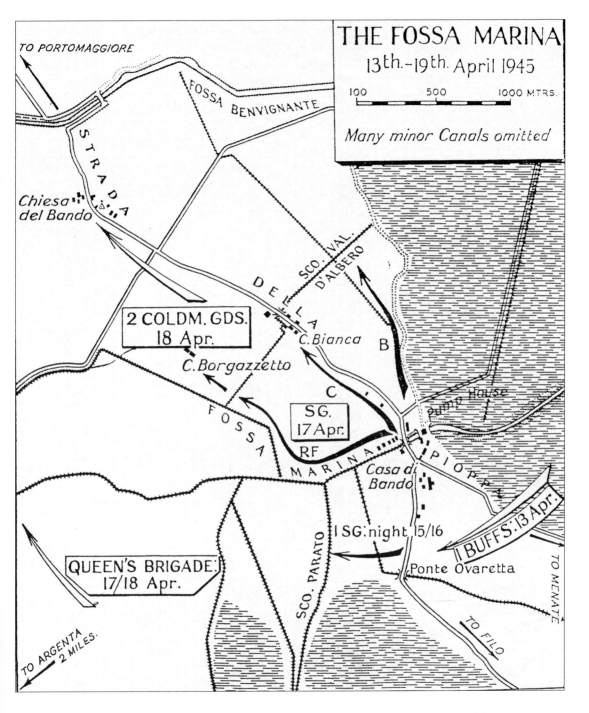

TO PORTOMAGGIORE

THE FOSSA MARINA
13th.–19th. April 1945

100   500   1000 MTRS.

Many minor Canals omitted

FOSSA BENVIGNANTE

STRADA

Chiesa del Bando

SCO. VAL. D'ALBERO

DELLA

2 COLDM. GDS. 18 Apr.

C. Bianca

B

C. Borgazzetto

FOSSA

C

SG. 17 Apr.

RF

MARINA

Pump House

PIOPPA

Casa di Bando

QUEEN'S BRIGADE: 17/18 Apr.

SCO. PARATO

I SG: night 15/16

Ponte Ovaretta

I BUFFS: 13 Apr.

TO MENATE

TO FILO

TO ARGENTA 2 MILES.

115

Bondo Pumping Station 2003

officer having swum across the gap to measure it, a very brave act.

No sleep tonight, this is now 3 nights!

17 April 1945 (Tuesday)

At about 0330 hrs we left our slit trenches on the road & proceeded in the order 10 Platoon & my Tac Coy HQ, 12 Platoon, 11 Platoon.

The plan being that 10 Platoon were to cross first & proceed to occupy the right hand corner of the field beyond, about 200 yards from the pumping station. 12 Platoon were then to make for the N.W. corner & dig in at the end of a factory by a road junction & if possible take a house the far side of the road known as 'Tiddler'.

11 Platoon were to follow 12 but strike due West along the canal bank & occupy the *S* end of the factory & the canal bank. I was a bit worried about 11 pln, but they turned out all right. Coy HQ was to be at the N end of the pump station building, unless I could find anywhere more suitable.

All went off as planned with the exception of rather an anxious wait of about 15 mins S of the bridge, in a much stonked area, while a platoon of LF got across & made their bridgehead. We were lucky & there was no shelling.

10 Platoon had a few casualties getting to their place, and a few more on arrival there from cup dischargers, mortars etc. 11 & 12 Platoons got their

objectives without much difficulty. We took about 10 prisoners & one or two killed. Sgt Copeland & Sgt Parkinson were both slightly wounded, & now L/Sgt Dudgeon commands 10 Platoon. Riley, Smyth MM, Dryden, Munro, L/Cpl Carson, Blogg and Watson, all got blasted, not badly except for Riley whose shoulder was badly shattered.

There was a certain amount of shelling & mortaring, but not as much as one might have expected.

RF under George Mann (just back out of hospital) went through us & cleared up the area known as 'Strong'. 'C' Company after a bit of a delay went on down the main road.

About 0800 hrs we were ordered to carry on down the bank past 10 Platoon for as far as we could go. We went about 300 yards before coming under fire from spandaus about 600 yards in front. We made as much progress as we could, but got held up just short of our objective, which was a small dyke. Sgt Rookbie was hit in the toe, & L/Cpl Watson got a bullet straight through his tin hat.

'C' Company were also held up on the main road to our West.

We had no tanks & could not advance against the spandaus dug in on the bank. We got behind a bend in the bank & dug in & remained there from about I p m until 9 pm. Only in communication by wireless, so could not get

Fosse Marina 2003

any news of tonight's plan, but gathered that 2nd Battalion Coldstream Guards would go through.

At about 9 p m, after dark, I was ordered over the wireless to mop up enemy positions to the line of the canal. I pointed out the difficulty of this & its probable cost in *life,* but was told it was absolutely essential to do this. Decided that the only thing to do was to send out a fighting patrol under Peter & give him a free hand to act as he thought best on the spot.

He went out about 1 a.m. & returned shortly, having had 2 men killed – L/Cpl Coull & Gdsm Wilson, both excellent men. He was lucky not to have had more. That was that, so we went to sleep again.

About 0430 hrs I was wanted by Col Ray on the wireless to put in a Company attack on the German position to clear up to the line of the canal. This was not on! So I ordered instead artillery & small arms fire at that area. I knew that 2nd Battalion Coldstream Guards were attacking sometime, but didn't know when. As it got light L/Sgt Nicholson & McFarlane went out to find that the Germans had gone. Italians also reported the place clear.

Everyone dead tired now having done 4 nights with no sleep. Col Ray came along about 10 a.m. & ordered us to follow along the bank a further 1000 yards to the line of the next canal. I took 11 Platoon only & A tac Coy HQ leaving the others to rest.

18 April 1945 (Wednesday)
The leading sections got very nearly up to the canal bank before being fired on by spandaus dug in the canal bank. They had to withdraw a little and we shelled the place a good deal. I brought 10 Platoon up under L/Sgt Dudgeon & put them in just in front of 12 Platoon along the bank, & about 200 yards short of the canal.

There we stayed until dark while LF were trying to work their way up the other side. The spandauing died down though we had Patterson hit at very long range. It started again at dusk, but it was quite obvious that the Germans were thinning out fast.

Col Ray came up before dark & said he wanted a patrol to go out to recce the canal bank. This I refused to do as the men were in no state to do anything about it at all. During the night 3 deserters came in who said the bank was clear. Col Ray did a recce on his own before first light, & we pushed 12 Platoon across the canal first thing in the morning.

19 April 1945 (Thursday)
A quiet & peaceful day & a good sleep last night, the first for 4 nights! Spent all day in the area & got a little more sleep & a wash etc. Italians say Boche have gone back about 10 kms. Men recovering slowly. Good heart considering all things.

Warning order to move came through late in the evening. We are to leave LF area at 0800 hrs tomorrow.

Total casualties: 2 killed, 15 wounded. Colin, Ian & LOB men came up.

We are about 20 men under strength in the Company. Hope we get a few days out to get ourselves properly re-organised, but doubt it, as the idea seems to be to push on as fast as possible.

20 April 1945 (Friday)
Had to move at 0800 hrs. to a forward concentration area S.E. of Portomaggiore. It was hoped we would stay the night there but this was not to be. We were ordered to move forward at about 1600 hrs at very short notice. Had rather a tricky 0 Gp in road N of Portomaggiore under shell fire, but this soon quietened down, it became apparent that the Germans were pulling out. RF followed by LF were to lead on down road & take Maiero & go past if possible. 'B' + 'C' looked like getting a quiet & comfortable night in Portomaggiore, where we got well dug in with beds etc. I had just got to sleep when was woken up with an order to move forward to another area just behind RF. We arrived about mid-night & the plan was for us to move off early the next morning at 0515 hrs. & with a troop of tanks to take 2 bridges about 2000 yards beyond where George Mann is.

The Company slept in the area of a farm-house. The house itself was full of Italians, so we had to disperse the Company around some haystacks etc. It was bitterly cold & we didn't get much sleep!

21 April 1945 (Saturday)
The tanks arrived at about 0500 hrs. & the company left about 0515 hrs. with 10 Platoon (Ian Fraser) riding on the tanks & the remainder in TCVs behind. The tanks had an 18 set which was supposed to be netted to us, but it didn't work & so communications were bad.

However we got the 2 bridges intact, though they were all ready for blowing + 2 prisoners + 1 killed + an ammunition lorry full of mines & explosives which blew up. This place was known as 'Radish'. I consolidated there by about 6 a m, but was immediately ordered to push on, which we did with some success, taking the next bridge 'Harico' at Ponte Azzano intact +2 prisoners & also the main bridge over the S Nicolo canal intact.

Here we had our first disaster of the day as 2 Spitfires straffed us & succeeded in killing one of the tank drivers & lowering morale generally, though none of our men were hit.

We were practically across the bridge & Sgt McPhail saw a lot of Huns swanning about who might have been put in the bag; but the delay gave them time to organise some opposition & a good deal of spandau fire & sniping.

We got 10 & 11 Platoons across the canal in the form of a bridgehead & were then rather stuck. Gdsmn Tinlin MM got sniped in the back. I hope he will be all right, but he is certainly out of the war. L/Cpl Butterwood (the L/Cpl stretcher bearer), was killed by a spandau firing from the canal bank.

Eventually after a long, and quite unnecessary, delay of several hours 'C' Company went through us at about 2.30 p m & carried on the advance taking about 30 prisoners, which I don't doubt we should have had if the RAF had not interfered.

We had our breakfast about 3 pm. Plenty of eggs in this area, & the civilian

119

population overjoyed to see us. After tea, clearing up the canal bank, we got a good many more prisoners, mostly Russians, making a total bag 33 for the day.

12 Platoon & Coy HQ pulled back into comfortable houses in Ponte Azzano. 10 & 11 Platoons were responsible for the canal bridge.

World news is that Bologna has fallen & the Russians are within 4 miles of Berlin, & that American & Russian forces have linked up, cutting Germany in two!

Had a quiet & comfortable night for once! Thank Heavens as the men were very tired & it was badly needed! L/Cpl Morrison was shot through the foot by that bloody fool, Murray, with a German rifle. Luckily he is not bad & ought to be back in 2 weeks or so.

Today's 3 casualties have all been men amongst the best we have got.

22 April 1945 (Sunday)
Moved off in TCVs soon after breakfast to secure a bridgehead over the canal at Veno del Rero, where the bridge had been destroyed, so that the sappers could put up a Bailey. Got the company across with some difficulty by means of a narrow girder, and a small boat which took only 1 man at a time.

Established ourselves quite comfortably the other side, the inhabitants produced quite a lot of eggs and an excellent non-alcoholic drink made of peaches.

Several prisoners, mostly Russians & a few Germans came & gave themselves up during the day. A couple in an ex-English 15 cwt, no doubt captured in the desert, drove into Sgt McPhail's platoon. Gerald Winter arrived up to command 11 Platoon in place of Jim Wilson, and Sgt Cormack to be pln sgt of 10 Platoon

As soon as the Bailey bridge was built, at about 4 p.m., the 27th Lancers went through, but met some opposition at Formignana & lost a scout car which was bazooked. They got to Coppara all right.

A good German half-track came back & we gave that to Hugh (Capt. H.N. Mansfield RAMC (Medical Officer to 1SG)

Another quiet & restful night.

23 April (Monday)
Coldstream went through us during the night.

About 10 am the Battalion moved to a concentration area between Formignone & Coppara, where about 12 reinforcements joined the Company, all very welcome after our casualties. About 3 pm we moved again to just this side of Coppara.

'C' Company were sent off to follow the Buffs & thence by a roundabout route to a bridge over a canal known as 'Nectarine'. Shortly afterwards LF left to go through the Coldstream on the other route to Nectarine. We were warned that we might be required to go through if LF got held up.

Slept until 0300 hrs when order to move came through. I was to go on immediately to Bn HQ. Remainder of Company to follow in jeeps & trailers supplied by Bde HQ.

24 April 1945 (Tuesday)
I went on ahead to Tac Bn HQ, on arrival found that the Germans had counterattacked LF & broken them up & disorganised them. 'C' Company were holding area of Nectarine. I waited for Coy to arrive & then went on up to Nectarine. Bridge was secure but situation rather tricky with a good many mortars etc flying about.

Got 10 Platoon into the buildings just S of bridge & Coy HQ & remainder of Company further back down the road. CSM Taylor got a lot of eggs & we had an excellent breakfast. Sent all C & LF men back. Decided that must hold buildings called Ghindarelli some 300 yards along road N of canal, with a view to (a) Getting sappers to repair bridge, (b) Going on to capture the next bridge known as 'Barkis'.

Got 10 Platoon under Ian to gradually infiltrate forward & this they did very successfully, but could not get into the houses which were strongly held. McFadzean was killed, L/Sgt Nicholson wounded & one or two others.

The sappers put some fascines in the hole, in the bridge, & we than had to wait for the tanks to return replenished with ammo etc. before we could put 12 Platoon & tanks through 10 Platoon under cover of 25 pounder smoke, to attack the buildings.

The tanks did not return until about 1 p m & we then launched the attack, at the same time I ordered Gerald Winter + 2 sections of his Platoon to go along the canal bank to the North & occupy the Germans there & if possible mop up some of them.

Only 1 Churchill tank got over the bridge, the next one toppled over backwards into the canal & the remaining heavy tanks couldn't compete at all. However the attack went well & 12 Platoon got into the houses in great style. 10 Platoon followed them up, & soon we had all 5 houses fairly secure, & a number of Germans killed & wounded, & 3 LF men rescued who had been hiding in the houses.

Almost at once 4 or 5 enemy S.P guns (at the time we thought they were M k IV tanks) opened up from the N bank of the wet canal only 150 yards away. Two of these were eventually knocked out by PIATs. Ian Fraser himself doing in one

Those 2 Platoons had to remain there for about 6 hrs. before the sappers had got the bridge passable for tanks, & this was a very tricky period.

Meanwhile 11 Platoon had had 5 killed & others wounded doing their job. I fear Gerald took it rather light-heartedly & many of the casualties were unnecessary. Total killed were: Gerald Winter, L/Sgt Mullen, L/Cpl Eastwood, L/Cpl Heap MM, L/Cpl Watson (died of wounds).

Company HQ & others had been doing a lot of Bren & rifle shooting at Germans on both flanks. Currie the sniper, whom I eventually got off Col. Ray, did well & shot several Germans.

It was a great small arms battle, & the first time I've seen our fellows using

121

them really properly, & giving back as much or more than they got.

About 8 pm the bridge was at last completed sufficiently for tanks to get over, but even then there was a good deal of hesitation & on arrival at the houses, where the Platoons were, they refused to tackle the one remaining SP gun, with the result that it got away.

1 platoon of RF had gone up to reinforce 10 & 12 Platoons + 1 platoon had come into my Coy HQ house, & as soon as it got dark George Mann took his Company up to relieve 10 & 12 Platoons who came back & we held a firm bridgehead around Nectarine. The stretcher-bearers did a magnificent job, mostly led by CSM Taylor who was quite fearless.

The company used their small arms with real effect.

Total casualties in the day: 1 officer (Gerald), 5 O.R's killed (L/Sgt Mullens, L/Cpl Heap MM, L/Cpl Eastwood, L/Cpl Watson, Gdsm McFadzean.

Wounded: L/Sgt Dudgeon, L/Sgt Nicholson, Gdsm Ivany, Dilling, Robertson, Davin, L/Cpl Bell, Lauder.

During the afternoon a German motor bicycle and side-car drove right up to our positions. We thought they must be a suicide squad trying to blow our bridge. 2 men were killed and the officer very badly wounded. He was brought in & spoke perfect English, said he had no idea that we were there and had been intending to visit some of his men.

Most of the men have now got watches & other loot!

25 April 1945 (Wednesday)

The Germans withdrew during the night to N of the R. Po & RF pushed on without any difficulty. The Bn moved up to area of Crespino during the morning on the S bank of Po. 'B' Company in rear in a field

The Germans have left a lot of stuff behind in their withdrawal including guns, motor transport and hundred of horses. Most of the horses are in very good condition, quite small, powerfully built animals. We held a company race meeting in the area in the evening.

O'Connor & I found a very nice German 3 tonner and Colin & Ian another one! Mine was driven by gas & had the distributor smashed, but this can soon be rectified.

The Queens Bde are across the Po & meeting very little opposition so it doesn't look as if the Germans can attempt to hold the Po. The Americans are well over and have captured Verona!

26 April 1945 (Thursday)

Saw the Brigadier at Bn HQ who said we were unlikely to move for 2 or 3 days owing to the difficulties of getting over the Po. Moved the company into houses in the village, none too soon, as it rained quite hard during the night, the first rain for months.

L/Cpl McMinn MM returned to the company from IRTD & a Gdsm Cassels joined us who I remember in 2nd Battalion Scots Guards. We are very much under strength. 10 & 11 Platoons with only 2 sections. No more men available.

27 April 1945 (Friday)

Ian & I went off in the jeep bound for Bologna, but Ian like a bloody fool drove it much too fast & had an accident & broke it up, luckily no one was hurt. We had to drive slowly back & visited Ferrara instead. AMG had closed everything including the cathedral, so it wasn't very exciting & we returned about 5 p m.

There was a Bn shooting competition run by Tommy Bulkeley, which we missed!

On the way to Ferrara we stopped & had a look at the 2 SP guns which had been knocked out by our PIATs. Both had neat little holes going right through their armour.

In the evening Colin & I walked up to see the Coldstream. Their Bn HQ are still S of the river, but they have 2 companies across who are having a very quiet time, no Boche within miles.

Saw Mike Hollings, Bob Clive, Ashley Ponsonby & Raoul Robin. They asked us to dine tomorrow night.

Said they had had 15 officer casualties.

They lost a complete company under George Gidney who took a wrong turning in their TCVs, & got in front of 78 Division among Tiger tanks & had to give in. 1 officer & about 12 men got back.

Alan Davidson's company has come up to replace them, and they now have only one complete company left at IRTD, so it doesn't look as if they or us can afford another blood-bath.

BBC news tonight said Bremen had fallen and the Americans and Russians had joined up 3 days ago.

Milan, Genoa, Turin in the hands of the partisans.

It looks as if what Germans are left are now in NE corner.

More rain during the night.

28 April 1945 (Saturday)

Some more rain.

Colin and I dined with the Coldstream and had a good dinner and cigar. Col. Billy in great form, but has changed his opinions of 56 Division! Alan Davidson has brought his company intact to replace George Gidney's people.

Spent very quiet day and wrote to the next of kin of all those who had been killed.

Order to move early tomorrow morning. The Battalion will cross the Po in Ducks and concentrate in an area E of Rovigo.

29 April 1945 (Sunday)

Had to get up at 0530 hrs. as some of the transport had to leave at that hour. Company left Cologna at about 10.45 hrs. to march about 3 miles West along the river bank to where we got ferried over in Ducks.

Masses of German equipment littered all along the bank of the river.

Interesting to see the old German pontoon bridges.

On the N. bank we had to wait for one and a half hours for the TCVs.

123

The River Po at Cologna, where hostilities ceased 2nd May 1945. Taken on the 8th May 2003

Dickie Westmacott turned up and I talked to him for a time. The Brigadier also turned up in great form. He told us Venice and Treviso had fallen, & thought we would do no more fighting!

Arrived at Battalion Concentration area E of Rovigo – not very comfortable, small and rather dingy houses, but plenty of eggs!

BBC reported Himmler offered unconditional surrender to America and England, but not Russia – offer refused!

<u>30 April 1945 (Monday)</u>
Heard that Mussolini and his mistress were shot in Milan by Italians and their bodies are on view!

NOTE: From 30 April 1945 'B' Company 1st Battalion Scots Guards continued to serve in the Trieste area until 28 September 1945. They then handed over their posts to the Italians and travelled by train to the Hook of Holland. The Battalion reached Pirbright on 2 October 1945, having been abroad for 4 years and 8 months.

'S' Company was reformed in 1971. It was attached to 1st Battalion Irish Guards and served with them in Belize. During that time they maintained the tradition of excellence set by their predecessors in Italy.

CHAPTER 12

The Qualities of Leadership

In the Second World War there were many incidents of outstanding leadership by officers, junior leaders and men. They have all been recounted and recorded in the various records and Regimental Histories. In researching the activities of 'S' Company and its worthy successor, 'B' Company, 1st Battalion Scots Guards, from March 1944 to the end of the War in Italy in April 1945, the records and various supportive memoires provided comprehensive coverage.

However, there was something different about this company. To say it was unique would, I think, be unjust, as I am sure there were very many other outstanding sub-units.

Careful analysis reveals that the men were meticulously trained, not only in the art of the infantryman, but also in the new concepts and thoughts of the Infantry Company in battle, put into practice after Dunkirk. Training can be very boring and dull, and much of it would be unduly repetitive and demoralising if up-to-date weapons and ideas are not incorporated to make it interesting and to give a professional edge. Here then was the re-birth of the Army after Dunkirk, where morale had to be raised and training had to be carried out as swiftly as possible to a very high standard.

This is where my story starts: the new ideas of the School of Infantry at Barnard Castle, which had to permeate down to Guardsman level. I have to say that I am not specifically qualified to comment on the leadership qualities of the two principal leaders concerned, Andrew Neilson and Richard Coke. All I can do is relay the judgement of others. This causes some imbalance as Andrew Neilson spent the best part of 2 years' training in UK before going to Italy. He lived only 4 months under wartime conditions to see the results of his efforts. Nevertheless, these efforts have been recorded and I have been able to pluck out various passages from letters and histories available.

Richard Coke was ideally placed to take over 'S' Company and was a superb choice. He had been with the 2nd Battalion at Salerno and later at the First Battle of Camino, commanding 'F' Company. There is considerably more to relate about Richard Coke because he was in the frame, so to speak, for a longer time. He was awarded the MC at Camino and after the amalgamation of 1st and 2nd Battalions, he was to remain in Italy, having been one of 2 officers with the least Mediterranean service.

Both Neilson and Coke were efficient competent leaders who were classified by their men as those who 'they would go for', the highest accolade. They were kind, considerate and absolutely fair in the way they took their men into battle. The men loved them all the more (love being a far deeper description than just respect for an officer) because they were of the breed who would not ask a soldier to do something that they were not prepared to do themselves.

The following letters and extracts paint the picture:

Andrew Neilson

To: Andrew Neilson
Part of letter from Lieutenant Col. Archie Douglas, CO Training Battalion, dated 15 December 1943

Pirbright Camp, Woking.

'I saw Lieut. Colonel today on my way through London and told him that I wanted you to stay (at Llandwrog) this time and that you had most unselfishly said you would.'

'Thank you, Andrew, for all you've done and for your present decision. You and Bill have been splendid and it will be a satisfaction to you to feel that you have taught so much to so many people. By your efforts the whole standard of training has been raised.'

Part of a Letter from Lieutenant Colonel Archie Pearson, Regimental Adjutant, dated 17 February 1944

RHQ, Scots Guards.

'You have had bad luck in being kept back when all your friends have already gone, but it may be some consolation to feel that you have been regarded as very nearly indispensable for so long. I have no doubt that there are many officers and men who have soundly cursed you (in secret!) but who have long since thanked their lucky stars that you taught them so well. The family and I send you our very best wishes and the best of good luck wherever you may be. If you ever have time do write a line and say how you are and how far the real thing compares with your dress rehearsals!'

Part of letter from Lieutenant Colonel Archie Douglas, CO Training Battalion, dated 31 March 1944

Pirbright Camp, Woking.

'My dear Andrew,
    Thank you so much for your letter. It is most encouraging to hear that the young entry, trained by you, Bill and Jack, have kept their enthusiasm so well. I

am so glad you have been able to band them together under you and hope they'll stay together and prove the value of what they have been taught. After all the School of Infantry puts out, it is high time someone put it into practice. It seems to me that they have the best opportunity of getting the information on which training should be based and of formulating the best tactics. Therefore one must accept and teach their ideas. If one is to do this successfully, one must go all out with no reservations. I think a lot depends on men, so trained, being handled by officers who thoroughly understand the system...'

Letter from Lieutenant Colonel Archie Douglas, Regimental Adjutant, dated 28 July 1944

Pirbright Camp, Woking.

'Dear Mrs Curtis,

I write to send you my deepest sympathy on the loss of your splendid brother, whose death has made all of us here very sad.

Of all the fine young men whom I have met in this war, I think Andrew was the most impressive. He had wisdom and judgment beyond his years. His activity and energy were unmatched. The men loved him. He was a real leader and he will never be forgotten.

I agree with L/Corporal Horwood, whose letter I enclose*, that he cannot be replaced. I had him for a considerable time under my command in this Battalion and in the 4th Battalion. I sympathise with you very much in your double loss.' (Double loss, because not only Andrew, her brother, was killed, but also her mother in the Guards Chapel bombing.)

*This described Andrew as 'a good officer and a fine leader'.

Part of a letter from Lieutenant Colonel R.E. Coates, CO 2nd Coldstream, dated 15 August 1944

2nd Battalion Coldstream Guards

'Dear Mrs Curtis,

This is just a line to say how terribly sorry we all are about Andrew, and inadequate as it must be to send the deepest sympathy of everyone in this Battalion to you.

He is a quite irreplaceable loss to us, as he was quite outstanding as an officer for drive, energy and courage, and the DSO he won on M. Piccolo was indeed well deserved, but besides all this he was a most charming character and a delightful companion.

We very much hoped he would recover, although he would have had to lose a foot (he trod on a schu mine) but the shock – which is such an incalculable thing – was too great, and I think too that coming on top of the shock of losing his mother had something to do with it.'

Letter from William Wynne Finch, Lieutenant Colonel, Commanding the Regiment, dated 6 September 1944

HQ, Scots Guards.

'Dear Mrs Curtis,

I regret that I was unable to write to you when your brother was killed in action as it was not till I arrived out in Italy that I learnt the sad news. I hope it may be of some consolation to you to know how everybody out in Italy spoke of the magnificent way he had carried out all the tasks that he was called upon to perform. When I was with the Army Commander he spoke to me about Andrew, praising the way he had always led his Company.

Now I am glad to say he has been decorated for that work and I only wish it had been allowed by Providence that he should have survived to receive that well earned reward in person.

Please accept my personal sympathy as well as that of the Regiment in your sorrow and loss of such a brave brother,

Yours sincerely,

William Wynne Finch'

Letter from Jack Messenger, Farmer/Landowner, dated 25 October 1944

Bonhams, Alton, Hants.

'Dear Mrs Curtis,

I am a complete stranger to you and for that reason I did not write, when I first heard of Andrew's death. For a stranger to write then seemed rather an intrusion. For about 2 years, Andrew came down to this place quite a lot, for training, and it was always a delight when he came. It was easy to forecast his innate leadership in battle and no surprise by his rapid promotion, he was a born leader and fighter. You must be very proud of having such a brother, and it is a tragedy that England too has lost such a fine man. His is the type that makes England great. The last time he was down, he was in Command of an OCTU, and when not training them, he had my gun and quested round the farm, for a little shooting. Jimmy Monteith often came with him and Lindsay-Peto. One can say little that really helps the bitterness of his death, but I lost my only brother at Langesmark in the last war, so I do understand of your grief with a deep understanding. Blois gave me your address, and he told me too of the double sorrow you have suffered this year, meeting death at such a time of prayer – makes me believe that a great purpose is being fulfilled, that is beyond our understanding.

Please do not answer this letter, but Andrew is so much in my thoughts, that I wanted to write to you.

His was a grand character and a charming man.

Yours sincerely,

Jack C. Messenger'

Part of letter from Lieutenant Colonel R.E. Coates, Commanding Officer 2nd Coldstream, dated 27 October, 1944

2nd Battalion Coldstream Guards.

'The Germans made 6 counter attacks (battle of M. Piccolo) most of which were badly knocked about by our artillery and 'S' Company's forward machine gun. They also mortared and shelled us and when they got close enough threw grenades and fired with their machine pistols and rifles.

Andrew walked about the whole time encouraging his men although he had been soon wounded in the arm. The Company fought like tigers, standing up and throwing grenades and shooting and finally lining up at 5 yard intervals and charging up the hill to drive the Germans back.'

Excerpt from *The High Road to England* **by Sir Ian Fraser, a Platoon Commander in 'S' Company and 'B' Company**

'The new company which I joined had had a remarkable history. 'S' Company had started life as the demonstration company at the Scots Guards Battle Camp in North Wales. The moving spirit had been their company commander, Andrew Neilson, a young captain and wartime soldier, who had been through the school of infantry at Barnard Castle. Neilson had carefully picked his 100 men from amongst the smartest and brightest of the recruits of two years and had filled them with ideas and enthusiasm. The reputation of 'S' Company was almost legendary when I joined them in August 1944. They had fought several difficult but successful actions on the way up from Cassino, which had earned them great esteem with their Coldstream colleagues. In the last of these actions Neilson had been killed and he had been replaced by a regular officer, David Cuthbert. He was the officer with whom I sailed out from Gourock the previous year and whom I so much disliked. When Cuthbert was torpedoed Richard Coke took his place. Colin Dalrymple, another scion of an old regimental family, was the very competent and acceptable second-in-command. But turnover amongst the platoon commanders was high, hence the need for me.'

Richard Coke

Excerpt from *The High Road to England* **by Sir Ian Fraser, A Platoon Commander in 'S' Company and 'B' Company**

'After a few days at Siena a message arrived from Richard Coke, who was now commanding 'S' Company about twenty-five miles away to the east, asking for a subaltern to take the place of John Lloyd-Johnes, who had just been wounded. The following day I found myself in command of No. 10 Platoon, 'S' Company, 2nd Battalion Coldstream Guards, 1st Guards Division, 6th British Armoured Division now part of the U.S. 5th Army under General Mark W. Clark. We were a Scots Guards company 'temporarily' on loan to the 2nd Coldstream to fill a gap caused by their heavy losses in the earlier part of the year. I spent the rest of the war commanding this platoon in the same company, always under Richard Coke.

Ultimately Richard became one of the two most highly decorated company commanders in the Regiment. He was a tall redhead, with a puffy, slightly angry complexion, a cadet then aged twenty-six, of the Leicesters of Holkham in Norfolk. The Coke family had been for centuries essential members of the English squirearchy and agricultural nobility and since the eighteenth century had sent sons into the Third Guards. The men resolutely called Richard 'Major Coak' – the family pronounce it 'Cook' – as I am sure their predecessors had always done. Without being in any way an intellectual he was highly intelligent and seemed to have a native understanding about what commanding an infantry company was about. A countryman through and through and a forester, he had a natural feeling for landscape and ground formation and knew instinctively what was militarily feasible and what was not. He puffed away at his pipe, never lost his temper, assessed the situation with rare acuity and the men loved him. 'We'll go for Major Coak,' they said. His officers, Colin Dalrymple, captain and second–in-command, Jim Wilson, John Inskip and I felt the same about him. He had that elusive military virtue, leadership.

It was not everybody that the men would 'go for'. The official histories and the memoirs of the commanders are silent on the subject but there was a good deal of not entirely unhealthy workers' co-management in the British Army in Italy at that time. If the men decided they would not 'go for' an officer, were he a platoon or a company commander, they let higher authority know in no unclear terms. Usually it was the senior NCO, the Company Sergeant-Major, who would march into the company office and, at a private interview, tell the company commander that Mr So-and-so was no good and that the men would not 'go for' him. Several company officers and even one battalion commander were, to my knowledge, torpedoed in this way. It was a strange, but on the whole very effective, style of man management.'

Address by Colin Dalrymple, Second in Command of 'S' Company and 'B' Company, at Richard Coke's Memorial Service

'Richard's father and mine served together in the South African War and World War I. But it was co-incidence that brought us together in Italy – we had not met before. I would therefore like to confine my words to our time together. I am making a tribute to him – not only on my own account but also on behalf of the men who served with him.

He arrived and joined 'S' Company, which was attached to the Second Coldstream on 26 July 44. We were in the Arno Valley not far north of Arezzo. I had been in the company for two months; thereafter, we were together until it all came to an end.

Disaster had struck 10 days earlier when in an attack just south of Arezzo, we had lost the lives of Andrew Neilson – the Company Commander – and Company Sergeant Major Brown, also seven other men. Andrew Neilson and CSM Brown held the DSO and DCM respectively. They were outstanding men and we were all shattered by their loss. Andrew was the third officer to be killed since the company had come out to Italy four months earlier and about twenty other ranks had died during that time. There was no sign of the war coming to an end and ahead of us lay a whole range of mountains, which the Germans seemed able to defend most effectively. Finding myself in charge of this depleted Company, I have to say that I was desperately worried and unsure of my own ability.

Richard's arrival was an enormous relief. From our time together in the Second Battalion Scots Guards, I knew of his capabilities and they were just what we required.

As has been reported in two excellent obituaries in the Times and the Telegraph, he had won the Military Cross on Mount Camino and we all knew about that. I had arrived on the day they returned from that action to an area about 10 miles behind the line in a dirty little village called Mondragone, about thirty miles north of Naples. I remember the sight most vividly even after some fifty seven years. I have never seen men in such a state of exhaustion, and, indeed, never did again. After about a week lying out in mud and rain, occasionally getting some rations and their essential tea, they were naturally unshaven, filthy; their faces were grey and they were worn out. Richard was amongst them and with, I believe, 56 survivors of his company which had started 105 men strong. His Company Commander was amongst those killed and Richard had taken over.

Richard continued to lead that Company – 'F' Company of 2nd Battalion

Scots Guards for the next three months while we crossed the River Garigliano and occupied a very dangerous sector of the front line. Not a major battle in terms of history but it cost the lives of our Commanding Officer and four others and an equivalent number of other ranks. By then the Battalion had suffered more than 500 casualties since landing at Salerno, Richard had accumulated valuable experience and had been lucky to survive.

With this background, Richard was exactly the man we needed for the job of commanding 'S' Company. He looked right, tall and strongly built, he managed to convey a special impression of seniority, which seems odd as I think he was only 26! He smoked a pipe, walked rather slowly with a walking stick and wore a black beret somewhat on the back of his head. He was a striking figure.

He behaved with confident authority. What he did and said always made plain common sense. He was immediately respected and trusted. The company recovered its composure, settled down and was able to face the obvious prospect of the remaining nine months of the war.

From the tactical point of view, he was well trained and knew what moves were reasonable and likely to succeed. If he thought that plans were ill-advised, he did not hesitate to say so.

The action on Monte Penzola rightly earned him the award of Distinguished Service Order. He deserved this for personal bravery but what I think is perhaps less obvious, is that it came about because of the support of his men – earned because of the way he had looked after them in the previous month.

He had maintained a high standard of discipline but it had not been imposed in a harsh way. At that stage of the war, living either in billets or the open air, had produced a special relationship between all ranks. Richard was, perhaps, unexpectedly kind and understanding of those who could scarcely bear the strain.

There remained the less spectacular but still costly action in the Po Valley – by the shores of Lake Commachio and then it all came to an end when we were just inland of Venice.

To end on a somewhat lighter note, on 2nd April 1945, the war in Italy had more or less come to an end. Richard, Ian Fraser and I had found a suitable place for the night in the village tailor's shop. Richard and Ian had settled down in their bedding rolls on the floor and I had been, I thought, rather smart and had got mine on the Tailor's counter. An Italian boy rushed by, I think on a bicycle, shouting 'E finita La Guerra! E finita La Guerra!' Immediately small arms firing broke out on a massive scale. Every Italian man at that time had some sort of firearm and claimed to be a partisan. The discharge of their ammunition was a long awaited celebration. Our field telephone rang and Ian Fraser answered it. 'The Commanding Officer' he said, 'We are to control the firing in our area.' 'Ridiculous, how can we' said Richard. 'Anyhow, he only said control it – not stop it.' And we all went to sleep. A small example of his ability to adjust to such problems.

Richard never failed on any of these occasions and without his guidance we would have had more casualties and less success. His contribution was immense and I know that I speak for all of us who took part. We were truly grateful to him for his courage and example which carried us through those very hard times.

Excerpt from a letter to the author from Professor Sir Michael Howard MC, which very aptly describes both Neilson and Coke

7 October 2003.

'I knew virtually all the officers that you mention, though none of them (except Ian Fraser) well. Having recurrent malaria (complicated by the jaundice that played such havoc with 'S' Company) I spent from January till July 1944 at the IRTD at Rotondi, where I was Training Officer to the Coldstream Company. I well remember the appearance of 'S' Company. It was very brief: I barely got to know Andrew at all, but remember him as a young man who took soldiering exceptionally seriously – not only soldiering but *fighting:* not quite the same thing. We all forsaw for him a DSO at the very least, and probably an early, very gallant death. I immensely envied him for being able to train an entire company from scratch, which was exceptional in Italy. Most battalions were made up of a few veterans from North Africa and a succession of drafts who came out at different dates from the UK, some of whom had been through the Barnard Castle battle-drill training and some had not. I had; but when I tried to introduce it at Rotondi the veterans who been in action since Tunis regarded the whole thing as absurd. That, they said, was not the way things were done in the Battalion!

Richard Coke was a dear, and your description is spot on. With his pipe and stick he looked like the gentleman farmer that he was, wandering round his estate, making sensible suggestions when necessary but leaving people to do their job in their own way. He was not someone who enjoyed war, but was jolly good at it. (I suspect that Andrew did rather enjoy war: I wish that more people on our side did!)'

APPENDIX A – Citations

THE DISTINGUISHED SERVICE ORDER
Lieutenant Andrew Shennan Neilson (219064)
Scots Guards

A Battalion of Foot Guards was ordered to carry out a night attack, crossing the start line at 0015 hours on 28 May 1944. It was ordered to capture and hold the Piccolo feature. Lieutenant Neilson commanded a company forming part of the Battalion and this company was directed on the westernmost high point of the feature. Lieutenant Neilson led his company with skill, speed and accuracy across most steep, difficult and enclosed country and took his objective. After daylight his company was counter-attacked and one of his officers was killed, but the enemy was repulsed and his company again held the crest. They were subjected throughout the day to mortar fire, sniping and grenades. Its flanks were frequently threatened by German infiltration, but by skilful manoeuvre and complete disregard for his personal safety while walking about to encourage his men, Lieutenant Neilson retained his objective.

At about 0430 hours Lieutenant Neilson was wounded in the arm but refused to leave his company until the position was stabilized at about 1100 hours, and in consequence lost a great deal of blood. After having his wound dressed at the Regimental Aid Post, Lieutenant Neilson returned to his company against the strong advice of the Medical Officer. Shortly after his arrival back with his company a strong counter-attack was put in by the enemy all along the Battalion position. Lieutenant Neilson again walked about in the open encouraging and manoeuvring his men until a near miss from a shell, and weakness from his previous loss of blood, caused him to faint twice and he was carried from the field unconscious.

There is no doubt that Lieutenant Neilson's skill, complete disregard for his personal safety and determination to remain with his company when wounded were major factors in enabling his company and consequently the Battalion to gain and retain its objective in spite of determined and prolonged assault upon it by the enemy.

MILITARY CROSS
Lieutenant H. F. G. Charteris
Scots Guards

The Coldstream Guards was ordered to capture and hold the Piccolo feature

6530, starting at 0015 hours on 28 May 1944. Lieutenant Charteris was 2I/C Company which was directed upon the westernmost high point of this feature. The company reached and held its objective but by 0430 hours one officer had been killed and the Company Commander wounded, leaving Lieutenant Charteris the only officer unhurt. The Company Commander refused to leave the battle until about 1100 hours, but through loss of blood was becoming progressively ineffective. Throughout a very exhausting day he controlled the company and organised the defence to hold the post against two counter-attacks as well as numerous raids; he had to direct the artillery and mortars, and also work the wireless as the signallers were wounded. Despite mortar and machine gun fire he went round the company position continually, and when the enemy attacked he was always there to take part in the very close hand to hand fighting with grenades and tommy guns. He continued until late in the afternoon when he was severly wounded in the head. The company continuously throughout the day put up a magnificent and successful fight against an enemy determined to regain Piccolo. Lieutenant Charteris's skill, example and courage was an inspiration to all and contributed largely to the defeat of the enemy.

MILITARY CROSS – immediate award

Capt. Richard Lovel Coke
Scots Guards
Mt. Camino.   Pt. 819.   9 – 10 November 1943.

This officer was 2 I/C of 'F' Company Scots Guards sent to the assistance of Nos. 2 & 3 Companies Grenadier Guards. The position was overlooked by the enemy and continually sniped and shelled. After the initial night attack this force became isolated and was compelled to fight its own battle. The Company Commander was killed and this Officer took command and displayed great gallantry, continually encouraging and leading his men over the most precipitous terrain. On Nov. 10th, these companies having suffered 70% casualties, it became necessary to regroup the force to hold a strong point. This Officer was entirely fearless, and showed personal leadership in selecting a fresh position whilst under constant M.G. fire. It was largely due to his courage and example that the position was held. Capt. Coke was in command of this company for 3 days during which they were isolated and under heavy spandau and mortar fire from three sides. When his company was eventually relieved he accounted for every single man to his Commanding Officer.

DISTINGUISHED SERVICE ORDER – immediate award
Maj. Richard Lovel Coke MC
Scots Guards
Monte Penzola

On the night of 4/5 Dec. 1944, 2 Coldstream Guards attacked and took Penzola (0523). The attack on the main feature Pt. 411, a pinnacle guarded by perpendicular cliffs, liberally mined, was carried out by 'S' Company under the command of Major Coke, Scots Guards. Major Coke led his company, under heavy shellfire which caused numerous casualties, round the west side of the cliffs to the rear of the enemy positions; an extremely hazardous operation as the Company was exposed on all sides to enemy fire and attack and it was unknown if the ground was passable. In spite of physical exhaustion due to the almost impossible ground, whose steepness necessitated crawling on hands and knees in some places and which was made still more difficult by slippery mud, Major Coke led his company to the assault. A fierce hand to hand battle ensued among the cliffs. Amid a hail of machine gun fire and shower of grenades, Major Coke succeeded in killing or capturing all the enemy. Fighting was particularly severe round the enemy Coy HQ where the German Company Commander and his HQ put up a desperate resistance in hand to hand fighting until he fell riddled with bullets, having caused numerous casualties among our own men. Major Coke was an inspiration to all during this fierce hand to hand battle and it was due to his leadership, spirit and determination that the attack was successful, an enemy company being destroyed and 1 officer and 25 other ranks being taken prisoner, many of them wounded. In spite of terrific and accurate shell and mortar concentration on the position, Major Coke now consolidated the position and, undeterred by the many casualties, prepared to meet the inevitable counter-attack. At 0530 hours on the 5 December, after severe artillery and mortar concentration on the position, the Germans put in a spirited counter-attack with elements of two companies. Using a tremendous volume of machine gunfire and grenades they penetrated to Coy HQ, where they wounded and killed several, including the CSM. Major Coke at this moment was a real inspiration to his company. Personally directing operations and throwing grenades in the close fighting, he beat off the repeated enemy attacks with heavy losses to the Germans. After the repulse of this attack, the Germans were unable to continue the assault. Major Coke's magnificent leadership, his complete disregard for his own safety under heavy shell and MG fire; his determination in the face of almost insurmountable difficulties in the terrain; and his heroic example had empowered his company to defeat a German brigade which from now on was powerless to challenge our possession of the commanding feature of M. Penzola.

DISTINGUISHED CONDUCT MEDAL
CSM Thomas Wright Brown (2754247)
Scots Guards attd 2nd Bn. Coldstream Guards

On 28 May, the Battalion were ordered to capture and hold the Piccolo feature. The Scots Guards company (attached to the Bn.) were directed on to the western high point of the feature and gained their objective shortly before first light. Throughout the day the company was subjected to heavy artillery and mortar fire, to sniping and attempted infiltration and early in the day all the officers in the company were either killed or wounded and evacuated. CSM Brown then took command of the company and handled it with such outstanding skill that the feature was held in spite of determined and prolonged assault on it by the enemy and in consequence the battalion was able to carry out its task of holding its objective. An officer finally took over from CSM Brown at night-fall.

CSM Brown's personal bravery in walking about under constant fire, his coolness in action and his capability of making quick decisions at critical moments of the day were an inspiration to all ranks.

DISTINGUISHED CONDUCT MEDAL – immediate award
Sergeant William Grant Young (2692927)
Scots Guards attd. 2 Coldstream Guards

This NCO was Platoon Sergeant to No. 8 Platoon when the battle for Point 501 (Monte Lignano) was joined on 15 July 1944. When the leading platoon was pinned down by heavy fire from entrenched German machine guns, he quickly organised his platoon into a fire position crawling about in the open along the crest of a small hillock and assisting in the siting of the Bren Gun positions. This covering fire enabled the leading Platoon to extricate itself into dead ground and the remainder of the company to form up for the assault. When the CSM was killed he became Acting CSM and later when a Platoon Commander casualty occurred he took over command of a platoon. During this time he showed strong powers of leadership and initiative and was an example to all. A piece of shrapnel from a 88mm shell tore the gascape on his back to shreds. Later when mortar bombs and shells were falling in our area, Sgt. Young crawled about the company encouraging the men, displaying great courage, cheerfulness and complete disregard for his own personal safety throughout the battle.

DISTINGUISHED CONDUCT MEDAL

L/Sgt. George Stussack Dudgeon (2698547)
Scots Guards

For conspicuous gallantry and devotion to duty in the Argenta Gap on 17 Apr 1945. 'B' Company made an attack at the Fossa Marina across the canal to capture some prominent occupied buildings on the north bank. Two previous attempts to force a crossing and establish a bridgehead had failed. Just as the attack started his Platoon Commander was wounded and L/Sgt. Dudgeon at once assumed command of his platoon.

In the face of heavy Spandau fixed lines and accurate mortar DFs this NCO led his platoon across 200 yards of completely flat ground known to be heavily mined and captured his objective. He successfully mopped up the buildings taking several POWs and beat off a counter-attack which developed just in the critical moment of consolidation.

Several hours later his platoon was ordered to advance in broad daylight to the next bund. Despite heavy and accurate Spandau and SP gunfire from about 500 yards range, which took its inevitable toll of casualties, he gained his objective by skilful use of the slight cover that existed.

During this action L/Sgt. Dudgeon, by his splendid example of personal bravery and devotion to duty, was an inspiration to his platoon. He rose to the occasion magnificently when his Platoon Commander was wounded and, despite the fact they they had had no sleep for the two nights prior to the crossing, he kept his men going for two more days under extremely exhausting and tiring conditions. He gained the confidence of all his men and was largely responsible for the success of his platoon.

APPENDIX B – Career Briefs Neilson and Coke

Captain Andrew Neilson, DSO

Andrew Neilson (ASN) joined up in the Kings Own Yorkshire Light Infantry at Strensal (as Pte 949206) to carry out basic training. In January 1941, he wrote to RHQ Scots Guards (Colonel E.W.S. Balfour) stating that he had recently been accepted by the Indian Office as a cadet in the Indian Army. He now wished to withdraw this application for compelling reasons and could he therefore apply for a Commission in the Scots Guards.

A rugby injury delayed his entry to Sandhurst. He joined The Royal Military College Sandhurst (61 OCTU – 14 platoon) on 9 August 1941. Granted Emergency Commission in Scots Guards 29 November 1941.

ASN was posted later to the Training Battalion at Pirbright and attended a number of courses: Messing Course London 2/42. Netheravon Mortar Course 10/3/42 – 2/4/42. Barnard Castle Battle Course 18/6/42 – 9/7/42 (graded distinguished). London District School of Tactics 30/8/42 –4/10/42.

Promoted Lieutenant on 1/10/42

Posted to 4th Bn. Scots Guards 25/1/42.

German Interrogation Course 11/5/43 – 15/5/43

Attached 3rd Bn. Irish Guards 5/9/43

Posted to Training Battalion Scots Guards 1/10/43.

He was at Warren Farm, Llandwrog for the period to 3/3/44 when he was posted to Italy, via ITRD, to 2nd Battalion Coldstream Guards, which he joined at San Potito 28/3/44.

Appointed Acting Captain 28/3/44.

Appointed Temporary Captain 28/6/44.

Died of wounds 16/7/44.

Had he not died from wounds in Italy on 16/7/44, it was known within the family that he would not have stayed in the Army after the war but would have gone back to Oxford to finish his Law degree. It is very sad that so many young men died in the War before their potential had been fulfilled.

Major Richard Coke DSO MC

1939: Richard Coke (RLC) joined the Supplementary Reserve of Officers of the Scots Guards just before the war started.

Early in September 1939 he was ordered to report to the Training Battalion Scots Guards at Pirbright Camp, Surrey as a 2nd Lieutenant.

He arrived there in civilian clothes, as it took a few weeks for his uniform to be made by a regimentally approved London tailor.

The Training Battalion Coldstream Guards was also at Pirbright, and the Coldstream and Scots Guards shared the officers mess (where the food was excellent).

Lt Col. Alan Swinton MC commanded the Scots Guards Training Battalion. Training proceeded with Drill Parades, Weapon training and a 1st World War system of trenches, Routes marched etc.

Many Reservists, both officers and other ranks, reported at Pirbright when they were called up. He was allotted one of these reservists, Guardsman H. Hibbert (a coal miner from Mansfield, Nott), as a soldier servant.

1940: On 16 October 1940 the 3rd Battalion Scots Guards was formed at Chigwell in Essex under command of Lt Col G F Johnson. RLC was posted as Signals Officer in Headquarter Company (commanded by Capt A.D. Murray) in this Battalion which formed part of the 30th Guards Brigade commanded by Brig. A H S Adair DSO MC Grenadiers Guards the other Battalions in the Brigade being the newly raised 4th Battalion Grenadier Guards and the 4th Battalion Coldstream Guards.

Before he could join 3rd Battalion Scots Guards he was sent on a Signals course at Catterick Camp in Yorkshire run by the Royal Corps of Signals, in January and February 1941. Before this some of the Training Battalion were stationed at Hurst Park Racecourse during the very hard winter of 1940 (The Thames froze over) and here, under Sgt. Parks he tried to learn the Morse Code and the rudiments of signalling including semaphore.

After Catterick he went to HQ Company 3rd Battalion Scots Guards in an old house called Rolls Park. The 4 Rifle Companies were scattered nearby at Buckhurst Hill and Chigwell. Training exercises were carried out endlessly, mostly in the Epping Forest area. As Signals Officer, he had to ride a motorbicycle (no fun in the rain and cold).

1941: At the end of May 1941, the astonishing news came that 3rd Battalion Scots Guards was to be converted into a Tank Battalion and that a Guards Armoured Division was to be formed.

Early in June many officers and other ranks were sent away on courses to learn from instructors in the Royal Armoured Corps about tanks. He went on a Gunnery course at Lulworth in Dorset (they were to have Cruiser Tanks).

In September 3rd Battalion Scots Guards moved to Tilshead Camp near Salisbury where it joined The Guards Armoured Division commanded by Maj-General Sir Oliver Leese Bt, and became part of the 6th Guards Armoured Brigade.

In November the Battalion moved to Codford 'B' Camp which was a collection of Nissen huts on the edge of Salisbury Plain.

1942: Meantime from about December 1941 – March 1943 he was sent as a gunnery instructor to the Guards Armoured Training Wing at Pirbright.

1943: In May 1943 the Battalion left Codford for the Hawes area of Yorkshire to train on the moors in their Churchill tanks which had replaced the Cruiser and Lt Col C I H Dunbar took over command of what was now known as 3rd (Tank) Battalion Scots Guards.

In June 1943 he was told by Col Claud (Dunbar) that he was to leave 3rd

Battalion Scots Guards, and go on draft to N Africa, meantime he would be transferred to Chelsea Barracks.

The draft left by train on 14 July for Glasgow, and embarked on the Moultain on 15 July for Algiers. Arrived at IRTD at Phillippeville on 30 July. Joined 2nd Battalion Scots Guards at Salerno on 15 Sept. There he caught malaria, and after a spell in hospital re-joined the Battalion in time for the First Battle of Camino 7 - 11 November. After this battle he was given command of 'F' Coy or what was left of it.

During training he was hit in the arm by a piece of metal from a PIAT (a new anti tank weapon). This meant another spell in hospital. Returned to the Battalion early in Jan 44, and was given command of 'F' Coy on 17 January. After nearly 1 month in the line in the Minturno area the whole of 201 Guards Brigade was withdrawn to Sorrento where 1st and 2nd Battalion Scots Guards were amalgamated, and a cadre of the longest serving personnel of 2nd Battalion Scots Guards was to go home, and reform.

1944: RLC was one of those officers detailed to go home. However, at the last minute and after 1st Battalion Scots Guards had been brought up to strength, he and one other officer, being the most recently out from England, were told they would have to stay, and were posted to the IRTD in early April. In mid-June he was able to get to Rome, and make contact with his two aunts one of whom had married a Marconi and had 3 children, his first cousins. This was the first of many happy visits to Rome, and many enjoyable parties when on leave.

Towards the end of July he was ordered to take command of 'S' Company Scots Guards which was attached to 2nd Battalion Coldstream Guards in 1st Guards Brigade. 2nd Battalion Coldstream Guards were then at Pontecino not far north of Arezzo. 'S' Coy took part in the slow advance to Florence over rough country, this entailed some fighting, and casualties.

They got to Florence early September 44, and were able to have a rest, and get to know some of the Florentine families and enjoy numerous parties. Coldstream Guards had been lent the Villa Ombrellino belonging to Mrs George Keppel, and Scots Guards took over the Villa Medici belonging to the Origo family.

Early October 1st Guards Brigade were ordered to take over a position in the area around Mt Battaglia from the Americans who had had heavy casualties. The positions were about 6 miles from the road where the lorries dropped them, along a steep, narrow very muddy track. The Battalion had to be supplied along the track by mules. Rain most of the time. They had some casualties from shelling, patrolling, and a German counter attack.

The winter was spent in various positions under extreme weather conditions: rain, snow and cold.

In early December 'S' Company was ordered to attack, and capture Mt Penzola which was the highest point on the Famosa Ridge. This was accomplished with fewer casualties than any of them had dared to hope.

On brief rests out of the line they went back to billets at Strada near Florence and the men and officers were able to take their turns to go on leave to Rome or Florence.

1945: From Jan 45 rumours started that 'S' Company would soon be leaving 2nd Battalion Coldstream Guards, and joining 1st Battalion Scots Guards who were in 24th Guards Brigade in the South African Division, and who had been engaged in heavy fighting in equally unpleasant conditions in the North West of Florence.

'S' Company finally left 2nd Battalion Coldstream Guards after a farewell Battalion Parade at Strada and embussed for Spoleto to join 1st Battalion Scots Guards and become 'B' Company.

24th Guards Brigade became part of 56 London Division and fought with them for the rest of the war through the bitter fighting in Lake Comacchio, and the numerous canals which had to be crossed in the Po Valley.

After crossing the Po the Germans collapsed and 1st Battalion Scots Guards went on to occupy Trieste where there was trouble with Tito's men, though fortunately fighting was averted.

Major Coke stayed with 1st Battalion Scots Guards in Trieste until October 1945. When Lt Col Claud I H Dunbar DSO came out to take over command from 3rd Battalion Scots Guards (The tank Bn) which had been disbanded.

Shortly after Col Dunbar's arrival, there was an incident in which one of 'B' Company's guardsmen, who had an excellent record up until then had a lapse and had to go up before the Commanding Officer at his orders.

Col Claud gave the man a severe punishment which Major Coke considered to be far too much. He told the Commanding Officer what he thought about it, and suggested that Col Claud have the man back, and reduce the sentence. Col Claud refused and so Major Coke said that he no longer wished to serve under him, and he asked to leave as soon as possible.

This was arranged, and after some home leave he took command of 'K' Company Scots Guards at the Guards Depot at Caterham, Surrey, for the remaining few months of his army service.

APPENDIX C

Routes and Dates of 'S' Company and 'B' Company in Italy 1944/5

1. Rotondi   20 March 1944
    Scots Guards Company at I.R.T.D. contained 400 fit men. 100 had arrived from Battle Camp in Wales.
2. San Potito   28 March
    1st Guards Brigade Joined 2 CG as 4th Rifle Company – named 'S' Company.
3. Cassino   5 April – 18 May
4. Monte Piccolo   26 – 29 May
5. Cerrano   5 June
6. Frosinone – Alatri – L. Canterno – Fiuggi – Genazzo 6 June
7. Montorotondi   8 June
8. River Farfa   9 June
9. Poggio Mirteto Station   10 June
10. Narni – Todi   11 June
11. Perugia   17 June
12. Monte Pacciano   22 – 26 June
13. Castiglio Fosco   1 July
14. Camucia   6 July
15. Lignano   14 July
16. Arezzo   16 July
17. Montevarchi   26 July
18. Cancelli/Rignano   4 August
19. La Torre/Villa Bonsi   6 – 7 August
20. Renacci   15 – 30 August
21. Pontassieve/Consuma   1 September
22. Dicomano/S. Godenzo   10 September
23. Villore   15 September
24. Peschiera   17 September
25. Monte Penna   22 September
26. Back to Arezzo   23 September
27. Back to Pontassieve   27 September
28. Up Sieve Valley   27 September
29. Pelago   2 October
30. Monte Battaglia   5 October
31. Battaglia West   15 October

32.	Casa Melina	24 October
33.	Monte Cornezzano	2 November
34.	Borgo San Lorenzo	12 November
35.	Castel del Rio	18 November
36.	Acqua Salata	22 November
37.	Castel del Rio (Res. Posn.)	29 November
38.	Penzola	3 – 4 December
39.	Penzola Ridge	8 December
40.	Relieved – to Rest Area	9 December
41.	Strada (S. of Florence)	12 December
42.	Return to Monte Verro and Acqua Salata	21 December
43.	4 more trips to Verro and Acqua Salata	(6 in all)
44.	To Spoleto	22 February
45.	Reorganisation/reconstitution	1 March
46.	'S' Company becomes 'B' Company 1st Bn., 24 Guards Brigade	15 March
47.	Ravenna pine woods	1 April
48.	Porto Garibaldi	4 April
49.	S. side of Lake Comacchio/Argenta	13 April
50.	N. Side of Fossa Marina/Longostrono	15 April
51.	Porto Maggiori	20 April
52.	Po di Volena/Formignana	22 April
53.	Copparo	23 April
54.	Cologna – Po War declared over at this point!	25 April
55.	Rovigo	29 April
56.	Final capitulation	2 May

APPENDIX D

Orbat of Officers in 'S' Company, 1944

1. At San Potito on formation   28 March

	Coy Comd.	Maj. H.D. Cuthbert
	2 i/c	Capt. A.S. Neilson
	Pl. Comdrs.	Lieutenant J.S. Wilson
		Lieutenant H.R. Bridgeman
		Lieutenant J.W.F. Lloyd-Johnes
	C.S.M.	WOII T. Brown

2. At Mt. Piccolo   26 – 27 May
Coy Comd.	Major H.D. Cuthbert – sick
2 i/c	Capt. A.S. Neilson
Pl. Comdrs.	Lieutenant J.S. Wilson – sick
	Lieutenant H.R. Bridgeman
	Lieutenant H.F.G. Charteris
C.S.M.	WOII T. Brown

3. After Piccolo
Coy Comd.	Major H.D. Cuthbert
2 i/c	Capt. A.S. Neilson – wounded
Pl. Comdrs.	Lieutenant C.J. Dalrymple
	Lieutenant J.E. Baxter
	Lieutenant J.S. Wilson
C.S.M.	WOII T. Brown

4. At Monte Lignano   8 July
Coy Comd.	Capt. A.S. Neilson
2 i/c	Capt. C.J. Dalrymple
	Captain J. Blackett Ord (temp.)
Pl. Comdrs.	Lieutenant J.S. Wilson
	Lieutenant I.J. Fraser
	Lieutenant J.H. Inskip
C.S.M.	WOII W. Young

5. At Reorganisation, Spoleto   18 March 1945
Coy Comd.	Major R.L. Coke
2 i/c	Capt. C.J. Dalrymple
Pl. Comdrs.	Lieutenant J.S. Wilson
	Lieutenant P.W. Bartholomew
	Lieutenant I.J. Fraser
C.S.M.	WOII T. Taylor MM

APPENDIX E
AWARDS

'S' Company
May 1944

Captain A.S. Neilson	DSO	Monte Piccolo
Lieut. H.F.G. Charteris	MC	Monte Piccolo
C.S.M. Brown	DCM	Monte Piccolo
L/Sgt. Jones	MM	Monte Piccolo

L/Corporal Downie	MM	Monte Piccolo
L/Corporal Smythe	MM	Monte Piccolo
Gdsm. Munday	MM	Monte Piccolo
Gdsm. Lingwood	MM	Monte Piccolo

July 1944

Sgt. Young	DCM	Monte Lignano
L/Sgt. McPhail	MM	Monte Lignano

December 1944

Major R. Coke	DSO	Monte Penzola
L/Corporal McMinn	MM	Monte Penzola
Gdsm. Rush	MM	Monte Penzola
Gdsm. Tinlin	MM	Monte Penzola

January 1945

L/Corporal J. Heap	MM	Monte Verro

As 'B' Company, 1st Bn.

March 1944

Lieutenant I.J. Fraser	MC	Po Valley
Lieutenant P. Bartholomew	MC	Po Valley

April 1945

L/Sgt. Dudgeon	DCM	Fosse Marina
Sgt. Allardyce	MM	Fosse Marina
L/Sgt. Moir	MM	Fosse Marina

APPENDIX F

Our Journeys in Italy, 2001 and 2003 – A battlefield tour

The whole story of 'S' Company (and later 'B' Company) made me curious to know more about them. The new training philosophy instigated after Dunkirk, whereby all the men with sensible battle experience (i.e. not the bravado types) within the army as a whole, were pooled together, was indeed worth pursuing. This led to new courses in weapon handling and tactics being developed at the School of Infantry at Barnard Castle, which in its turn gave birth to individual battle camps. These were run by regiments at various outlandish locations to provide what we called continuation training in the 1960s and 1970s.

The Scots Guards had such a location at Llandwrog in North Wales, and it was here that all the various thoughts on tactics and weapons came to a head.

One of the most important subunits is the infantry platoon and all energies were used in N. Wales to perfect the tactics of this subunit. The art of Bren gun, grenade and bayonet close quarter battle drills was a key factor in the success of 'S' Company. Many courses of recently trained young men went through Warren Farm to end up at Rotondi in Italy (ITRD)

Andrew Neilson, my uncle, was one of the young officers who trained these men, and such was his (and others') prowess at producing just the right mixture of sheer guts and will power, with a high level of competence, that made 'S' Company such a success. My uncle was of course keen to get to grips with the war, but was held back to continue this training initiative. There are letters held here that show that eventually in late 1943 he was allowed to go – and all of these letters were most complimentary on his ability.

To me, it made a lot of sense, as a retired officer, to find out more about what went on in Italy. All I had was a copy of Erskine (given to my mother by CSM A.Croucher at an open day at Mons Officer Cadet School, when I was a cadet) and what documents I discovered after my mother had died.

The first journey was aimed at following in my uncle's footsteps, from Naples/Rotondi to his grave at Assisi. Not much attention was paid to the various encounters except perhaps Mt. Piccolo, just north of Cassino, where my wife and I went over much of the ground. However, we found Rotondi, a dirty little town north-east of Naples, near Benevento, and followed the route up to San Potito, where 'S' Company joined 2nd Battalion Coldstream Guards. We covered the road to Cassino and tried to imagine going into the line at the dead of night and having to traverse Mad Mile. After Piccolo, my uncle was in hospital for some 10 days, which was followed by some sick leave. He rejoined just after Perugia.

We made a complete mess of Monte Pacciano and it was only discovered and visited on our second journey. The preparations for Monte Lignano at Arezzo are well related and again we had approached the objective from entirely the wrong direction. It was only with a marked map from Colin Dalrymple that we were able to take the time and get to the objective on our second trip.

Our first trip ended with a visit to Ossaia, the RAP where my uncle died of wounds having stepped on a Schu mine. A visit to his grave in Assisi brought the whole story to – then – a very sad end.

However, having written up Piccolo in the Scots Guards Magazine of 2002, I felt that I now had to complete the story. Needless to say, I received much encouragement to do so from all quarters, and another visit to Italy took place in May 2003. We flew to Rome, hired a car and made Spoleto on the first day. The next day we searched for various points mentioned in the various histories. We failed to find the Opera House or any of the locations associated with the amalgamation. We did however search for the large house or orphanage at S. Martino in Trignano. We found what could have been it about 4 miles west of Spoleto. This building was named Villa Matignano in No Dishonourable Name, and described as a house which does not possess a single passage. We took photographs of it to try to confirm our supposition.

After Spoleto we paid a visit to my uncle's grave at Assisi, again, and then set out to find Mt. Pacciano. As already described, we couldn't find it on our first visit, but on the second we found it and photographed it from a point slightly higher and more to the west than that shown in Gdsmn. Leaf's drawing in No Dishonourable Name. In fact a very good view can be had from the suburb of Perugia called San Marco. Our next port of call was Arezzo, where we found a superb villa hotel facing the northern slopes of Mt. Lignano. After a splendid meal and a good sleep, we set off next morning, with Colin Dalrymple's marked map, which really was a great help. We had, as I say, got it all wrong 2 years earlier. We now had the direct route of 'S' Company through Battalion Tactical HQ to the objective. We took this to be just west of S. Anastasio. Having probed up every lane from the main road from Il Matto to L'Olmo we believe we came across this line of advance. In any event, at any point in our search, I estimate we were no further than 150 yds. from this line. We then set off from Arezzo up the old road in the Arno valley, passing through some place with familiar names, such as S. Leo, Ponticino, Montevarchi, S. Giovanni, and Renaci. As 2nd Battalion Coldstream Guards were to spend their rest and recuperation time out of line at Greve in Chianti, and Strada, we turned left into the Chianti hills, and visited both of these towns – now summer retreats for the wealthy and holiday centres for visitors (mainly Dutch).

It was in Strada, on 21 February 1945, that a farewell parade was held, firstly, to bid farewell to Major General Murray, who commanded 6 Armoured Division and, secondly, as 2nd Battalion Coldstream Guards was leaving 1st Guards Brigade and, finally, for the Battalion to say farewell to 'S' Company.

We then got back into the Valley and spotted S. Mazzano on our way to Pontessieve and Fiesole, where we spent the night. The next day was to prove to be the hardest in that we had to get over the mountains before nightfall. Again a string of familiar towns were passed as we made our way to the Grogo Pass – Rufina, Dicomano, Borgo S. Lorenzo. At the point where the German Gothic line crossed route S610 we came across a monument to the US 5th Army, at a point called Mt. Attuzzo, to commemorate the breakthrough on 13-18 September 1944. Firenzuola marked the start of our journey down the

Santerno valley, where we stopped at Castel del Rio to check our bearings. There is a large hill east of the town with a castle, which we initially took to be Mt. Battaglia, but after a bit we decided it could not be it.

This then just left us the task of finding Mt. Penzola, which from existing maps looked totally isolated and without access. However, after some pretty deductive map reading we found a road which crossed the Santerno at Fontanelice and wound its way up into the hills. Having passed through the hamlet of Monte le Pieve, we arrived at a farmhouse at Gesso. Here the farmer's wife and her son took us to behind the barns and there spread out above us was Penzola. From the hand drawn map in Erskine, we were able to get our bearings. These mountains were white/grey in colour and different in colour and texture to Battaglia just across the valley. We were even able to identify a winding gully with a track in a prominent position which we assumed was Colin Dalrymple's track!

After spending the night in Faenza, we tackled Monte Battaglia next day, via the spa town of Riolo Terme. Further up into the hills there is a circuit of reasonable roads leaving Casola Valsenio, which took in Arugno, and S. Ruffillo. At the top we suddenly came across prominent signs which led us to the top of Battaglia, which is now identified as a centre of military importance and a nature reserve. Having read the reports of the fighting and graphic descriptions of knife edge ridges it was a surprise to get almost to the top in the car. There is the castle, adorned with old sculptures and there are of course several suitably inscribed memorial tablets.

After the horrific incidents in the mountains, 'S' Company with 2nd Coldstream withdrew back to Strada and thence through the territory they had spent the best part of the previous 12 months fighting for. They arrived at Spoleto, where both the 1st and 24th Guards Brigade came to rest. They were reorganised and 'S' Company became 'B' Company 1st Battalion Scots Guards.

Having sorted out Monte Battaglia it was time to move on into the Po Valley proper and experience a new type of terrain. Very like Lincolnshire, but with more trees – the Po Valley is the centre of the peach growing industry, and they also grow kiwi fruit. First stop was the pine woods at Ravenna, where we stopped for lunch. The woods are today punctuated by open camping spaces and restaurants, but it was easy to imagine the semi security of bivouacking here.

On proceeding north down the Spit, we saw on our left a large expanse of Lake Comacchio, which is about half the size of 1945. Even so there are still today large expanses of marshy areas which must have been much the same in 1945. Porto Garibaldi, the objective, is today a thriving collection of Marinas with expensive yachts and beaches. It is – in atmosphere – a cross between Southend and Cowes. There was very little to see to give us any idea of how the incident progressed, save that it must have been wet and insect ridden.

We followed almost exactly the route taken by the Battalion, south of the River Reno, and skirting the flooded area then called the Wedge. We naturally did not expect to see any remnants of wartime activity but there were certain important points. We passed through Langostioni and Menata and spent time in the area of Bando and Fiorana. We wanted to find the Pump House, and found a building in what appeared to have been the correct place at Bando, called Casa di Bando in 1945. It was astride a big canal which we took to be the Fosse Marina, but a number of waterways had obviously been changed.

From Argenta we went on to Portomaggiore, Roverelto, Finale di Rero, Coppara and eventually arriving at Cologna, where war was declared over in April 1945. Both my wife and I feel rather empty now that the exploration was over and considered that it was thoroughly well worth doing. It has highlighted somewhat the 15 months' existence of a company of men fighting in enormously difficult terrain. The fact that a Scots Guards Company joined another Guards Battalion, 2nd Coldstream, went to show the flexibility of war-time soldiering. In operations which in the main were the task of individual platoons – the fact that the arrangement went so well was a credit to all concerned.

During this visit to Italy we had not decided to visit any of the Commonwealth War Cemeteries, except my uncle's at Assisi. However, the cemetery in the Santerno valley is quite magnificent and we found two chaps who were well known – Lieut. Lumley of the Coldstream Guards and Pte. Linwood MM of the Scots Guards. We also had a quick look at the Faenza cemetery, where we found L/Corporal J. Heap MM and later decided on the spur of the moment to visit to cemetery at Argenta Gap. It was very much a quick decision to turn off the main road, and yet again we found one of those strange incidents that one so often has – the third grave we came to was Captain T. Lindsay-Peto MC, who was one of my uncle's great friends. Ian Fraser describes brilliantly his last moments with a mortally wounded Tim Lindsay-Peto in *The High Road to England*. Within a few moments we came across the graves of Gerald Winter and D.A. Colquhoun, killed in the last days of the war. Overall, a shattering and emotional visit, having read about and 'got to know' these young officers during the previous year.

APPENDIX G

A chance meeting with Mr Peter Ellis, retired Scots Guards, at Woking, August 2003

Sometime in late July, Major Edward Crofton, Regimental Adjutant, Coldstream Guards, gave me the name and address of a retired Scots Guards Sergeant living in Woking. I rang him up, as he was one of the stretcher bearers who had brought my uncle down from Mt. Lignano on 15 July 1944.

Mr Peter Ellis kindly agreed to see me at his house in Woking on 6 August. He is 80 years old and had joined the Scots Guards in 1938, as a Junior Soldier, at the age of 15. He was in fact trained as a Drummer and served in the Band. In 1943, at the age of 20, Ellis, like many others found himself at I.T.R.D. Rotondi and was drafted off to 'S' Company as a stretcher bearer. His normal location would have been in the area of Company Headquarters, ready to move with his team to collect the wounded.

He remembers very well the activities on 15 July and recognized various features of North Western Lignano from photographs that I had taken during my last trip to Italy. 'S' Company, together with 2CG, had moved forward on the night of 14 July and lay out on the lower point of the mountain (probably near Il Matto). In darkness, the Grenadiers mounted the attack and by midday 'S' Company were moving to carry out their part of the attack. It was at this point that my uncle trod on a Schu mine and was mortally wounded.

Ellis and 3 others were sent up to bring him down at what must have been mid-afternoon. He remembers getting to the scene and that it took them 4 hours to get him down to the R.A.P. Ellis was at this point unclear what happened then – but he felt that my uncle had died at the R.A.P. – in fact he was given a blood transfusion at the Advanced Dressing Station and evacuated to No. 2 Casualty Cleraring Station, where he died in the early hours of 16 July 1944.

Ellis, even at his age, could remember reasonably clearly much detail of these 2 days. He was kind enough to say that my uncle always led from the front and that 'S' Company would do anything he asked of them.

APPENDIX H

Visit to Warren Farm, Llandwrog, 18 – 19 August 2003.

The one last link in the story of 'S' Company was the Battle Camp at Warren Farm. As the first draft of the book was doing the rounds, I drove north with Major Jim Kellie from my Regiment to see the site of the Farm and the Camp. I had first made contact with the current owners, Mr and Mrs Tommy Budgen, who suggested that I could put up a notice in the pub and local shop to trawl in interested parties. On 18 August, we arrived at Llandwrog, having visited Carnarvon Cemetry, where we found the grave of Guardsman Duncan, aged 19, who died in 1946.

Mrs Budgen was most charming and showed us the site of the Camp, which was between the Farm and the beach. There is some sort of hollow in the dunes, which had the foundations of what could had been the Nissen huts, together with a water tower. Not far away, near where the entrance track came in, was a typical World War II pair of buildings, which were, I expect, the Quartermaster Stores and MT yard.

The entrance track is still visible and where it entered the Nissan hut area there is a prominent concrete slab, into which had been set a collection of white pebbles in the shape of the Scottish thistle. This is recognizable, even after 60 years, and the layout of the Camp was with some imagination also recognizable.

Warren Farm, itself, has been much improved since the War and is the Budgen's holiday home. It is remote to say the least and it did not take much to imagine the winter gales blowing off the sea. Similarly the inner creek is easy to recognize as one of the best wildfowl shooting areas in North Wales.

We concluded that the Farm must have been the Officers' Mess and Camp Office and was some 200 yds from the Main Camp and the QM block.

Later in the day, we had an appointment to meet a Mr Peter Hughes in the pub, as he had seen my notice and rung me up. He was 17 in 1943 and remembers well the goings on in the area. Sometime earlier an airfield had been bulldozed and tarmac laid, south of Warren Farm, where the RAF trained navigators and air gunners. He went on to say that the first residents of the Camp were the Tank Corps, who did not stay long. The village was regularly visited by RAF personnel, but the Scots Guards tended, with a few exceptions, to keep themselves to themselves at the Camp.

Hughes said that the beach was mined and he remembers 2 Guardsmen

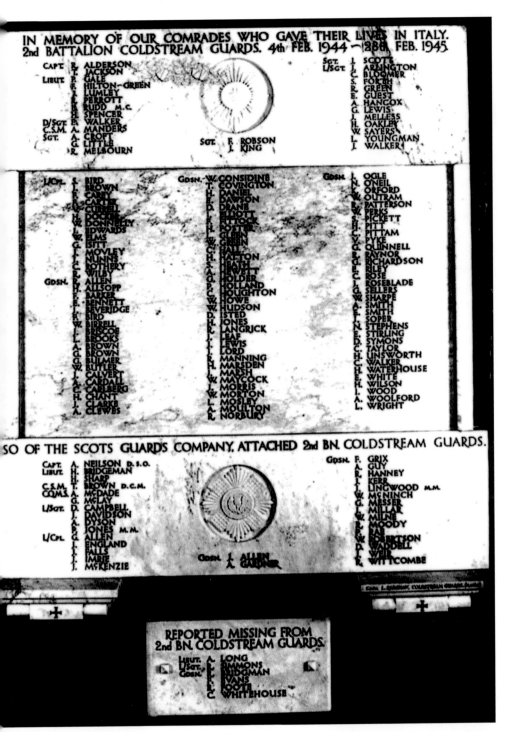

The Coldstream Guards War Memorial at St Mark's Church, Via Maggio, Florence, 2001

being killed in some sort of accident. Whether it was grenade training or by the mines he was not sure. He does remember that there was a Captain Woods at the Camp, who lived with his wife in the village – he could have been some sort of Camp Commandant from another regiment. Mr Woods collected money for one of the Guardsmen to be sent home for burial, which may account for the one lonely grave at Carnarvon.

Hughes also stated that the Menai Straits area here had Coastal Battery guns on the shore. These emplacements were blown up in 1980 by Mrs Budgen's brother, as they were becoming unsafe.

It appears that at the end of World War II the complete stockpile of nerve gas bombs produced by Hitler (TABUN) were removed from Germany, to stop them falling into Russian hands. 71,000 bombs were deposited on Llandwrog airfield – and it was when Hughes noticed some of them weeping that they were removed. About 12 DUKWs loaded these bombs into a cargo ship offshore, where they were taken and sunk into the North Atlantic.

The locals seemed to remember that the Battle Camp existed well after the War, which may explain the grave of Gdsmn Duncan in Carnarvon in 1946.

APPENDIX I

Letter from Richard Coke regarding the morale of guardsmen

Officer Commanding,
2nd Battalion Coldstream Guards,
CMF.
Reference letter dated 8 December 44. Request from AFHQ

Points affecting the morale of guardsmen

1. PAY The guardsmen and the ordinary infantry soldier are the lowest paid men in the Army. They have undoubtedly one of the most dangerous jobs in the armed forces and a considerable amount of discomfort to put up with often over long periods. At the same time they see other men in the Army drawing higher pay with much easier, more comfortable and safer work. This does not make for high morale, on the contrary, it makes for discontent and must surely be wrong.

There is at present no incentive for a man to volunteer for the infantry. The fighting troops in the front line, whoever they are and to whatever Regiment they belong, deserve special considerations, and one of these should be considerably higher pay than those behind the line.

At present it is often the case that the further back from the front line you go, the more pay you get, e.g. Staff and Corps pay. It ought to be the other way about.

2. *TROOPS* A short time ago the official figure for Army troops in Italy was 400,000. We had 8 divisions and various independant brigades (these figures may be wrong, but the point remains) fighting in Italy. By no means all the men in a division are *fighting* men. This means that all the fighting is borne by a very small percentage of the total strength of the Army.

Those that do the fighting, in addition to drawing far higher pay (as is suggested in 1 above) should also have some special distinction in uniform, e.g. some badge or medal which should be highly prized. A divisional sign does not meet the case. The badge or medal may be on a company or battalion basis and awarded to those who do well and should be capable of forfeiture should the unit do poorly at any time.

3. *AMENITIES* More amenities could be available just behind the front line for the fighting man. At present ENSA, etc. are apt to stay in the rear area.

It is very noticeable that troops in the back area in complete safety and usually comfort always have plenty of beer, etc. (a commodity which sometimes is not seen for long periods by fighting troops).

4. *INEFFICIENT PERSONNEL* At the present time it appears regrettably to be the fact that those officers and other ranks who are inefficient in their jobs in the fighting line are often promoted to more highly paid jobs in the rear area. It is suggested that this is not good for morale.

5. *REGIMENTAL UNIFORM AND DESIGNATIONS* There are a large number of officers and other ranks in the Brigade of Guards and doubtless in all other Regiments in the Army who are fit, not over age and have not served in action with their Regiments, and appear to have little intention of so doing if they can possibly avoid it.

It is a scandal that these people should be allowed to walk about in the uniform of the Regiment to which they have contributed so little. Such people should be transferred to the General List.

6. DESERTION   If the powers that be wish cases of desertion to cease or at any rate be minimized, then action should be taken on the preceding paragraphs and punishment of desertion should be amended as follows:

Anyone convicted of desertion should be shot. If popular opinion will not accept this then:-

It should be made known that deserters will have to serve in special penal battalions in Burma or some other such part of the world where amenities are bad.

R.L. Coke, Major
Commanding,
'S' Company (Scots Guards)
attached 2nd Battalion Coldstream Guards
10 December 1944
Copy to Regimental Adjutant, Scots Guards.

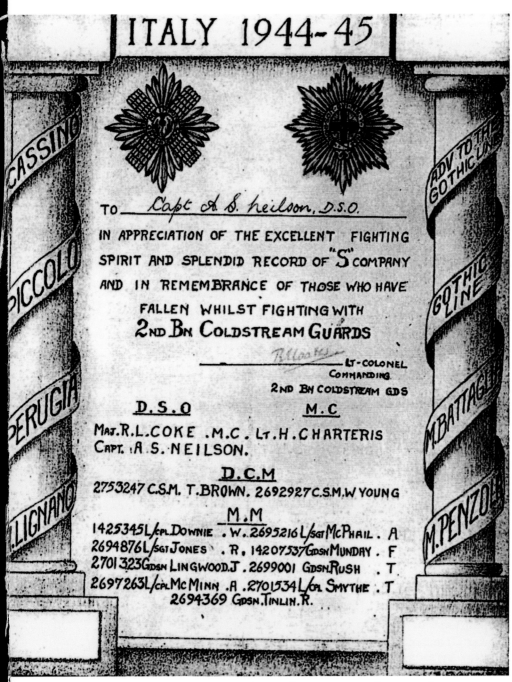

ITALY 1944-45

TO _Capt A S. Neilson, D.S.O._

IN APPRECIATION OF THE EXCELLENT FIGHTING
SPIRIT AND SPLENDID RECORD OF "S" COMPANY
AND IN REMEMBRANCE OF THOSE WHO HAVE
FALLEN WHILST FIGHTING WITH
2ND BN COLDSTREAM GUARDS

LT-COLONEL
COMMANDING.
2ND BN COLDSTREAM GDS

D.S.O   **M.C**

MAJ.R.L.COKE .M.C. LT.H.CHARTERIS
CAPT. A.S. NEILSON.

D.C.M

2753247 C.S.M. T.BROWN. 2692927 C.S.M.W YOUNG

M.M

1425345 L/CPL DOWNIE . W . 2695216 L/SGT McPHAIL . A
2694876 L/SGT JONES . R . 14207537 GDSN MUNDAY . F
2701323 GDSN LINGWOOD.J . 2699001 GDSN RUSH . T
2697263 L/CPL McMINN .A . 2701534 L/CPL SMYTHE . T
2694369 GDSN.TINLIN.R. . . .

*The card presented to all members of S Company by Lt Col R E Coates,
Commanding Officer 2nd Battalion Coldstream Guards*

Index